30 Secrets of Success in Marriage

A Book for Premarital and Marriage Counseling

30 Secrets of Success in Marriage

A Book for Premarital and Marriage Counseling

Prof John Gatungu Githiga

Copyright © 2021 by Prof John Gatungu Githiga.

SECOND EDITION

All rights reserved. No part of this book may be reproduced in any form or by any electronic or mechanical means, including information storage and retrieval systems, without permission in writing from the publisher, except by reviewers, who may quote brief passages in a review.

ISBN: (Paperback Edition)
ISBN: (Hardcover Edition)
ISBN: (E-book Edition)

Book Ordering Information

Phone Number: 315 288-7939 ext. 1000 or 347-901-4920
Email: info@globalsummithouse.com
Global Summit House
www.globalsummithouse.com

Printed in the United States of America

OTHER BOOKS BY THE AUTHER

The Spirit in the Black Soul

Christ and Roots

Initiation and Pastoral Psychology

Ministry to All Nations

FROM VICTORY TO VICTORY

DEDICATION

This book is dedicated to my father and mother, Isaac and Joyce Githiga and my father –in-law and mother-in law Hiram and Joyce Kahungu for honoring their marriage vows and for staying together in marriage until they were parted by death. And to Bishop Neville and Vera Langford-Smith, First Bishop of Nakuru, a celebrant of our Wedding, who ordained me Deacon and Priest and faithfully ministered in Tanzania and Kenya for over forty years and for staying together in marriage until they were parted by death.

ACKNOWLEDGEMENT

I am most grateful to my dear wife, the Rev. Dr. Mary Githiga for being the most faithful companion and helper and to all those who have revealed their secrets of success in marriage and to Isaac Cyprian Githiga and the Rev. Dr. Waterhouse for proofreading the manuscript.

CHAPTER

INTRODUCTION

1. LET THE PATRIARCHAL BE THE PATRIARCHAL
2. LET THE MATRIARCHAL BE THE MATRIARCHAL
3. DON'T BE BOSSY
4. LOOK FOR A STICKER
5. MUTUAL RESPECT
6. NEVER ALLOW ANYONE TO COME IN BETWEEN
7. MUTUAL LOVE
8. FOCUS MORE IN STAYING MARRIED THAN IN GETTING MARRIAGE
9. LET HIM BE HIMSELF AND LET HER BE HERSELF
10. KEEP AND TRAIN
11. LOVE FOR THE LORD AND THE MINISTRY
12. CHRIST AT THE CENTER
13. PUTTING UP WITH EACH OTHER
14. HUMOR AND HARD WORK
15. FRIENDSHIP
16. A HUNDRED PER CENT DEAL
17. A GIFT OF VIRGINITY

18. A GOOD SEXUAL RELATIONSHIP
19. FARM AND CHILDREN
20. CHASE HIM/HER
21. DETERMINATION
22. HOLDING EACH OTHERS HAND
23. COMMUNICATION
24. WE DON'T USE SILENCE AS A WEAPON
25. NOT PERFECT BUT TENACIOUS
26. OUR OPEN SECRET
27. PLANT THE SEED OF THE GOSPEL GOLDEN WEDDING ANNIVERSARY
28. NURTURE YOUR BEST SELF
29. CAUSES OF FAILURE IN MARRIAGE
30. REARING CHILDREN IN A TECHNOLOGICAL SOCIETY
31. FOR THOSE WHO INTEND TO MARRY
CONCLUSION

INTRODUCTION

The knowledge of the secrets of success in marriage is of vital importance since no institution is as challenged as the marriage institution. In United States fifty per cent of the marriages end in divorce which has devastating effect on children. Africa and other countries are not excepted. The marriage enrichment seminar which I held In Kenya identified the following as the challenges*(changamoto)* which are facing the marriage: poverty, infertility, lack of mutual trust, adultery, lack of communication, misunderstanding, rejection from the parents of the spouses, finance, lack of transparency, violence, drunkenness, addictions, lack of marriage counseling or one of the spouse going with a wrong company.

In the following pages we will focus on the secrets of success in marriage. Being a pastoral theologian, I will start from the case and then move to the Holy Scripture. I have learned that any success in marriage can be supported by the word of God. Since this work started when I was working as a chaplain in the USA, most of the people whom I interviewed are in North America.

Over the years I have been intrigued by huge success of 50 per cent of the marriages is North American. As a clergy who has ministered in this country for many years, I have been astonished by the way these marriage partners have devoted themselves to their marriage and the ministry. As I give pastoral care in the Hospital, I have been astounded by the way they care for each other in sickness and death. Most of these couple grew up during the great depression and are rightly known as the builders. They are indeed the one who laid a firm foundation in the United States. I have said jokingly, "if there is anything like human cloning, I would like this age group to be cloned".

I have, however, found it wise, to interview them and ask them one simple question: "what the secret of success is?' The question often brings a twinkle in their eye. They have openly and generously shared their stories. I have also shared with then the secrets of success and fruitfulness of our marriage. Most of the time our discussion is so interesting that they don't want us to part.

This book is about the secrets of success in marriage. It is also about the success in life and in human relationships. Some of the secrets are intriguing and interesting. Some of my interviewers have said: "This have worked for us, it may not work for others." There are some of the principles which have worked for a particular personality types which may not work for other types. But there are those which are fundamental to all marriages. We are going to start with those which are not obvious particularly in the society which is regarded as a patriarchal.

The last chapter of the book draws from numerous marriage seminars I held in Kenya. The group ranged from one hundred to seven hundred. Rather than lecturing them, I engaged them in discussion. The question for discussion was: "What destroys the relationship between a husband and a wife?" (For more information see my book: *Initiation and Pastoral Psychology*

p.133-144.). in all the seminars there was heated

discussion. I still remember a man standing at the rear seat of 700-members church who said: "We are experiencing a pull between two teachers-traditional and modern." The tradition drew from the wisdom of a patriarch society while the modern draw from a society in transition which was becoming both patriarchal and matriarchal. Interestingly, the American couples who I interview reveal that American families are both patriarchal and matriarchal.

It has also to be noted that the couple may start as patriarch in the morning of their lives but become a matriarch in the afternoon of their lives.

CHAPTER ONE
LET THE PATRIARCHAL BE THE PATRIARCHAL

Jay and Mary have been married for 58years. They were given a first prize at their granddaughters wedding for being the longest in marriage among the people who attended the wedding. Jay, who was in sickbed, holding my left hand tenderly stated that the secret of their success is "she does whatever I tell her." "Do you also have "honey does"? I asked. The wife who was smiling answered for him: "he does, but I do more than he does." She justified that he is the head of the family. "But more importantly," responded the husband, "we have God on our side and we have each other." The wife consented by holding his hands and giving him a winsome smile.

Jack and Janie have been successfully married for 42 years. Jack who was in the sickbed believes they have been together because each one knows her role. "I deal with big thing; she deals with small things." You sound as though you are the head". I reflected. "He is the head." The wife confirmed. "But I am the neck, and I am the one who turns the head."

If you are the head, the Bible admonishes you to love your partner as Christ loved the church and gave himself for her, to make her holy, cleansing her by washing with water through the word, and to present her to himself as a radiant church, without stain or wrinkle or any blemish, but holy and blameless." You have to regard your wife as your crown and joy. You have to love her and make her feel loved. When you take Christ model, you will not regard your wife as your servant. Remember our Master said: "For the Son of Man did not come to be served, but to serve, and to give his life as a ransom for many." Mark 10:45

CHAPTER TWO
LET THE MATRIARCHAL BE THE MATRIARCHAL.

An Anglo husband who was married to the same wife for 54 years was the most out spoken: "The secret of our success is two words" "which words?" I interjected. "As big as I appear (he was 7' 2" she was 5' 2") we have stayed together because of two words: "yes Mom." The wife who didn't deny that she is the head of the family. Added: "We have had a good marriage and never had any major disagreement."

Another white couple who had a winsome sense of humor had been married for 62 years. The husband was in a sick bed while his wife stood by him with expensive cream suits. The wife quickly told me about their secret. "I beat him a lot." "You are kidding." I responded "She is not kidding." The husband responded. "I allowed her to gain the upper hand early in our marriage." Do you have another secret?" Yes", responded the wife." We like having fun and traveling together. We have been in many cruises. My husband says that I am the expensive one."

I was amused by another couple who have been married for 54 years. The husband said: "The secret of our success is that I must have last word" "You sound autocratic." I teased. "No. you didn't let me tell you what my last word is." "What are your last words?" I queried. "My last words are: 'Yes dear.'"

A widower who was married to the same wife for 48 years and who spoke so highly about her revealed the secret of their success: "I allowed her to get it on her way. She was the matriarchal."

Another interesting testimonial of female leadership was given by a daughter who was visiting her 94 years old mother who told me that her mother was married to the same man for 74 years. This middle-aged woman who has been successively married to the same husband for 54 years said: "My dad was a laid back and easy going. But my mother was a tigress. She was the leader of the family and whatever she said that was what was done. She tried to rehabilitate me; but it didn't work because I am very much like her. I have been married for 54 years. My husband and my children know that I must have the last word. My three sisters are very much like me. They are matriarchal. I enjoy leadership. The other day I was holding conversation with my 42 years old son in which my son finished with 'Yes Mom."

The other day I met European American at Discount Tire. While we were waiting for the repair of our tires, I introduce myself to Jack. "Are you married?" I asked. "Yes." He responded with a feeling of fulfillment. "How long have been together." We have been married for sixty-two years." "What has kept you together?" I queried. "Two words: Yes Mom." Early in our life, I decided that I better win her to myself rather than winning the argument. I also allowed her to lead the family and take care of the children. When we married she was working with the school, but when we got children, I asked her to quit her job and stay with children. We now have two grown up sons who have successive marriage." "Is there any other secret?" I asked. The other secret is that my wife is the only person who can put up with me." Jack also wanted to know how long we have been married and when I told him that we have been married for forty-two year he responded: "Keep that woman".

We learn from Jack and his wife that the road to success is respecting the leadership; to prefer to win the partner rather than the argument.

The above testimonies which come from the Americans of European descent who are considered patriarchal attest to the fact that leadership in the family is not a role of a one gender. Among the African American whom I passionately ministered for 12 years, the majority of the leaders are female.

A research which was done in Kenya revealed that owing to absentee husband, who go to the town to make a leaving, 60% the mothers are in charge of day to day leadership in the families. This has and will continue have effect on married partner. At one occasion during premarital counseling, the husband to-be said to his faience: "I come from a single mother family and I am accustomed to my mother's leadership. So, lead and I will follow."

During marriage seminar which I facilitated in Karura Parish in Kenya, I young wife commented: "I used to be bothered by my husband for not playing the leadership role, but eventually, I resolved to regard him as one of my boys. I am however aggravated whenever he disobeys." This young woman was both a leader and a bread winner and so she expected her leadership to be taken seriously.

Is there Biblical evidence of women leadership? Just as there were men in leadership, there were also women leader.

Despite living in predominantly patriarchal society, Deborah was the head of the state, command in chief and chief justice and prophetess Not only did she summon her General, Barak but she also accompanied him in the battle. (Judges 4:5-31). Communication between Deborah and Barak is interesting: "Barak said to her, 'if you will go with me, I will go; but if you will not go with me I will not go." And she said, "I will surely go with you, nevertheless, the road on which you are going will not lead to your glory, for the Lord will sell Sisera into the hand of a woman". Deborah being a prophetess, not only she predicted the victory but also that Jael, a woman will kill Sisera, Jabin's General. The narrator portrays Jael as a matriarchal. Her names come first: "But Sisera fled away on foot to the tent of Jael, the wife of Heber" (Judges 4:17). And Jael the wife of Heber took a peg of the tent and took a hammer in her hand and went softly to him and drove the peg in his temple, till it went down into the ground, as he was lying from weariness. So, he died."

As we have argued about patriarchal, if you a matriarchal you have to love your husband as Christ loves the church. Honor him. Appreciate him. Respect him. Serve him. Use Jesus as your model. In the Gospel of John, we are told "Having loved His own who were in the world, he showed them the full extent of his love......After that, he poured water into a basin and began to wash his disciple feet." John 13:1-5. If you love your husband as Christ loved the church he will stick with you.

If you are head of the family, avoid being autocratic. A story is told of a matriarch who lived with her adult son and the husband. On one occasion she called both men and asked them to quickly check what was burning in the kitchen. The two men were preparing to leave and each were dressing. As the mother was issuing the order, they had to decide as to whether they have to defy or run to the kitchen naked. They opted to defy and the matriarch. And of course, she took care of what was happening in the kitchen. If you are the head, be reasonable. Even God invites us to reason to with him. "Come now, let us reason together, says the Lord." Isaiah 1:18. Avoid issuing two orders at the same time or unrealistic demand as King Saul ordered David to bring his two hundred foreskins of the Philistines.

CHAPTER THREE
DON'T BE BOSSY

Asked about the secret of the success in marriage, Elaine answered: "My husband would say that the secret of success is to never allow your wife tell you which room you have to start vacuuming." If your chore is to vacuum the house, don't let your wife tell you that you must start either from room 1 or from the kitchen. If she is a matriarch, do not encourage her to be bossy. One of my house chores is to take out the garbage. In the house we have trash cans. I wouldn't allow my wife to tell me which garbage I can must starting emptying. And when I am driving, I need freedom of driving. Sometime when I am drive 70 mph in 75mph road, if my beloved tells me to slow down, I may increase the speed. On the other hand, when my wife is cooking, I don't regulate the way she cooks. It is up to her to decide whether she would start by preparing vegetables or **ugali.**

At one occasion when I was ministering African to Americans we were invited by a matriarch. The husband complained to me: "I wish my wife would stop ordering me in the presence of our guest." Later on, the Matriarch accompanied me to a mission to trip to Congo DR. We were given a ride from the airport by a bishop who drove decisively and aggressive fully. The matriarch shouted: "Slow down." The bishop who had little English shouted back: "Me, Dr Mengi driving!" "We do not want to die." The matriarch shouted back. The bishop accelerated and shouted back: "Bishop, Doctor, professor Mengi driving. Die go to heaven!" He never reduced the speed but we arrived Kimbangu Center safely.

There are also Patriarchs who are bossy. There is a family story which my mother narrated with lot humor. This happened long before I was born. My Father and mother had spent long hours working in the farm. They returned late in the evening and father ordered the mother go to the river to get the water for washing the baby. The river was about a mile way. Mother was too tired to comply. Father became physical. The mother and the elder children fled to her parents and left the father with a baby. He has now to take care of the baby and the animals. After two days of complex chore he went to look for mother. Being a preacher, his next sermon was directed to him. He repented. "I will never beat my wife again." By protesting mother gained her dignity. More often than not, freedom is never given; it is taken. But in marriage, it has to be taken with love and forgiveness. According to Kikuyu mythology, the community started as a matriarch. But eventually the wives became ruthless. To solve this problem, men held a meeting. They all agreed that they are going to make love with their wives and make them pregnant. When they were all pregnant, the husbands overturned the government peacefully.

Thus, if your partner is bossy. Liberate yourself, but with love. Remember what St. Paul says about love: "Love is patient, love is kind. It does not envy; it does not boast, it is not proud, it is not self-seeking, it is not easily angered, and it keeps no records of wrongs. Love does not delight in evil but delight with truth. It always protects, always trust, always hopes, and always perseveres." I Corinthian 13:4-6 Someone who truly love will stick to his/her partner.

CHAPTER FOUR
LOOK FOR A STICKER

Mark and Joyce had previous marriages which were terminated by the death of their spouses and are in 11th year of their second marriage. In their second marriage they were looking for a sticker. "Someone who can be with you for better for worse, for richer or poorer in sickness and health till death do us part." Their decision was not based on what feels good but what is right.

How do you get a sticker? Know about your friend before you decide on marriage. Know that the past behavior predicts the future behavior. If your friend had had several broken relationships, it is more than likely that he is someone who runs away from obstacles. This implies that after marriage, when challenges arise, he will desert you for a wilderness which has no problem. And of course, this wilderness does not exist. More often than not, the quitters are a part of the problem. They are drifters. They are like the dry leaves in the sea shore which are drifted by the current. Said differently, the drifters always see the green grass on the other side. But they never make effort to make the grass greener where they are.

To get a genuine sticker with whom you can build a healthy relationship, you have to look for someone who is in Christ. This is not just someone who goes to church. He/she has to be a person who is in Spirit. Who bear the fruits of the Spirit which is love, joy, peace, patience, kindness, goodness, faithfulness, gentleness and self- control. Galatians 5: 22-23. If both of you are in Spirit, then there must be a mutual respect.

CHAPTER FIVE
MUTUAL RESPECT

An Anglo couple who has been married for sixty yours stated that their secret of success is mutual respect. This indeed is the secret of much successful marriage. To be respected one had to command respect for the very meaning of the word respect is a feeling of deep admiration for someone elicited by their abilities, qualities and achievements. Mutual respect is the very meaning of genuine love and hard work. You cannot expect respect if you are a deadbeat. For instance, a husband reported how he was beaten by his wife. The cause of the fight was that he came home drunk and went to bed and at night he urinated in bed. His wife who was awakened by urine beat him up. You cannot disrespect your spouse and expect respect. Malcom X talking about respect said: "Be peaceful, be courteous, obey the law, respect everyone, but if someone put his hands on you, send him to the cemetery." Respect requires hard work and self-discipline. And to be courteous to your spouse. It is by respect that you win your spouse to yourself. "To command respect, you have to work hard to improve yourself. Respect your effort, respect yourself, self-respect leads to self-discipline. When you have both firmly under your belt that is real power." Clint Eastwood. Thus, if you want to have a fruitful marriage you have to respect your marriage partner. As Paul puts it "outdo one another in showing honor" Roman 12:10. This entails letting the other partner get the credit. This implies that you will "do nothing from selfishness or conceit, but in love *count other better than yourself . . . This implies that: "you will not only look for your own interest, but also the interest of"* your spouse. It was this attitude which cemented the relationship of the Anglo couple mention above. This will also hold you together: "till death do us part." If you hold this position you will not allow anyone come between you.

CHAPTER SIX
NEVER ALLOW ANYONE TO COME IN BETWEEN

A widower who had been married for 63 who lost his wife a year ago emphatically said: "We never allowed anyone to be between us. We also loved each other as though the only thing which we had was each other. We also worked hard and lived below the means. Our philosophy was "Just do it!" and live a day at a time. This couple reminds us what the Bible says: "therefore *a man leaves his father and his mother and cleaves to his wife, and they become one flesh." "Genesis 2:24 and* for that reason the two can be together naked without being ashamed. Our Lord even laid greater emphasis on oneness: *"and the two shall become one flesh. So, they are no longer two but one flesh. So, what therefore God joint together, let no man put asunder. Matthew 19: 5b-6.*

It can be argued that it is ok to love and respect parents, and other family members and friends, but you should never allow any of them to poison you against your partner. Your partner is a part of your very self, and so to hurt him/her you are hurting yourself. Remember your partner constitute more than 75% of your environment and for that reason if you pr!otect her, you are protecting 75% of your environment. You are indeed protecting your body and your image.

CHAPTER SEVEN
MUTUAL LOVE

A husband who has been married to the same wife for 39 years had this to say: "She is my first and last wife. We have been married for 39 years. We met in restaurant and then dated for two weeks and they married. Our secret of success is mutual love, mutual respect and mutual help." More than half of the people I interview agreed that it mutual love was the major secret of success. They also affirmed that not only do they love each other but they liked and enjoyed each other.

You too can learn to love and like your partner by seeing her as the most important person in your life. When it is difficulty to love her/him remember most cherished moment in your life. Your first date and wedding day and honey moon. And then view her in light of that moment. One wife who has been with same husband for 51 years told me that her secret of success was that she learned how to love her husband when he was most unlikeable. This means that you have to love your partner even when she is depressed and when she sees everything in negatively. This is indeed the time when she demands you love and care. You have to cherish her and love her dearly.

Anglo couples who have been married for 55 years believed mutual respect rather than love was what bound them together. The wife had this to say about her husband who was a Judge: "He didn't know how to love or express love. This is something which he learned later. What kept us together in the early stage of our live is respect for each other and ministering in the church and the community. We started a program of at risk kids and we fostered many children. We now have ten years an adopted daughter. ''People always asked me whether she is my grandchild" remarked the Judge, "I tell them no. She is my sister." But both of them have to learn the words "I love you." 'We now can say to each other: 'I love you.' And we also tell our children and grandchildren: "I love you."

This couple was speaking for so many couples included my wife and me. We started with mutual respect and ministering together and unarticulated love. This is what we inherited from our parents. We never heard them say either to us or each other "I love you". They however expressed their love with deeds. I still remember my father expressing his love for me when I was a little boy. I was playing outside when he called "Gatungu! Come and pinch a stone." Running in the house he gave me a cup of fresh milk. It was love of God which made it possible to for Mary and me to tell each other: "I love you" and say the same to our children. And our children expressed the same to us.

More than 40% of the people I interviewed stated that love was the secret of their success. A wife who was caring for husband had been married to the same husband for thirty-five years, emphatically stated: "Our secret is a four-letter word: LOVE". And another couple who have been married partners for fifty-three years revealed their secret: "love and share values."

A clergy couple who were married for sixty years and served God for forty-one years maintained that the secret of their success was love for each other and ministering together. Love cements the marriage and helps you to enjoy each other because: "Love is patient, love is kind. It does not envy, it does not boast, it is not proud. It is not rude, it is not self-seeking, it is not easily angered, and it keeps no records of wrongs. Love does not delight in evil but rejoices with truth. It always protects, always trusts, always hopes, always persevere." Love allows your partner to be and to become.

CHAPTER EIGHT
FOCUS MORE IN STAYING MARRIED THAN IN GETTING MARRIAGE

I was with three Anglo American at Walmart where were waiting for our vehicles to be serviced. One of them reported what his pastor said during the wedding: "The major causes of divorce is that the partners put more energy and resources in getting married than in staying married." This pastor had made an accurate observation. While in the US this entails expensive bachelor patty and wedding reception, in African and Asia, it entails expensive dowry and wedding reception. I was discussing this issue with an Indian couple who had been married for sixty-six years. They informed me about how marriage has been commercialized in India. The parents of the girl (unlike Africa) are required to pay the dower to the parents of the bridegroom, and the charge is in accordance to the education the young man. If he has a Master' degree the charge is higher if he has a doctorate the price is even higher. And if girl change he mind and refuse to marry the young man, he is burned life.

Moreover, there are other crimes which are related to dowry, for instance, a recently married women can be a target for dowry related violence because she is tied economically and socially to her new husband. In some cases, dowry is used as a threat or hostage type situation, in order to extract more property from the bride's family. This can be seen in new brides, who are most vulnerable in the situation. Dowry crimes can occur with the threat or occurrence of violence, so that the bride 'family is left with no choice but to give more dowry to protect their daughter the northern and eastern states of show higher rates of dowry-related violence.-

In Kenya and other African countries, the bride is regarded as a community. In some cases, the parent of the girl asked for money or love stock which live the couples impoverished. In one case, the dowry and wedding party left the couple with no money for rent. Consequently, they were evicted and then lost their job and went to live with the parents of the bride groom. The other case was of a young man who visited the home of his girlfriend with a helicopter. The bargaining team set the price so high. The young man was so disgusted and left the team, jumped in his helicopter and flew away and the girl friend committed suicide. So, the parents lost the bridegroom to be and their daughter.-

The battle against the commercialization of marriage need to be fought the community. This include parents, pastors, as in the case of the one who preached against it. Even thou the bride and bridegroom are venerable, the should join hands. I had a golden time of interviewing a young Muslim woman who sat with me as we were flying from Dubai to Kenya. I asked her about the dowry during the arrangement of her married. She said: "My dad asked for KS 500,000. I then said to him: 'Dan! All what I need is a Koran and a prayer mart. Please do not ask for that money. Eventually my Dad asked for Ksh150,000." I asked her a second question: "when you knee on the mart and pray and read your Koran, how do you feel." Bishop this is a difficult question but I will try to answer. I feel positive energy."

This lady gave us the answer about what is needed in marriage: "Positive energy" This is what the Bible refer as the fruit of Spirit which is: love, joy, peace, patience, kindness, goodness, faithfulness, faithfulness and self-control. Galatians 5: 22-23.

So, if you are intending to marry, you can talk to his parents if they are exploitive. Remember you are a human being, not a mechanize. You need to be faithful to God and avoid cutting the cake before the marriage. Be in Christ and God will protect and provide for you. Mary and I are witnesses of God's guidance of provision. We were both committed in ministry. We attended church camp where we were taught about the friendship between boys and girls. We attended early morning prayer. Mary was in the choir and was the one who was giving the tune. We regularly attended weekly Bible study. When we started courting, all our dating was held in the city park. Our loving Father protected us from exploitation. During dowry negotiation. Before the bargain my mother in law became my defense attorney. Her opening statement was: "remember they will need food after the wedding. My father in law spoke out: "The only thing that I need is a pair of shoes. That was within my reach. The wedding party team led by Pastor David Waweru, mad it as economic as possible. The party costed only Ksh270 which was my one-month salary. Wedding cake was provided by Ann Ball, a British missionary. Bridal vehicle was provided by the Bishop Langford Smith. For our honey moon, we had Presbyterian Manson. This was provided by the Rev Ian Patterson who was a Scottish and with whom we started a company of Boys and Girls which became the mother of Brigade companies in Kenya. Ian left us with his cook who provided us with bedroom coffee.

During the reception we were given so many gifts which included money and so we started with enough cash.

So, our advice to the unmarried who plan to marry is that be faithful to God and to one another. Commit yourself to Christ who is the way and the bread of life, and he will guide and provide for you. He will give the fruit of the Holy Spirit. He will make you magnanimous which will make you enjoy your differences. That is- you will allow each other to be.

CHAPTER NINE
LET HIM BE HIMSELF AND LET HER BE HERSELF

An Anglo couple who have been married for 41 years stated that the secret of their success was the discovery and accepting that they were two different individuals. And so, they agreed from the very beginning that they will allow freedom of expression of their individuality. "We greed that each one has to be who he/she is and that we must agree to tolerate each other. And love each other as distinct individuals.

This is important message for the reader whether you are single who is looking for a marriage partner or married and you are trying to form your partner in your own image and likeness. You need to let the other partner to be herself. And the other side of the coin is that you both have to learn to compromise. The "strong one should not try to swallow the "weak" and the "weak" should strengthen herself/himself so that he is not a slave of the viewpoint of his/her partner. One man who has been with the same wife for 45 years and whose children had problem in saving their marriages stated that that "When two are coming together, they are like two Canyons (ranges). They must struggle to make the bridge. They are also like two trees on the two canyons which must form a bridge. There must be overwrapping between the two trees in order to make the bridge strong. That is each one must sacrifice something and compromise something." As a married partner you have to learn how balance between your individuality and communality, between "I" and "we" and how to compromise without losing your individuality.

CHAPTER TEN
KEEP AND TRAIN

I was amused by an Anglo couple who had been married for 60 years. They married when she was 16 and he was twenty. They both agreed that the secret of their marriage was keeping and training. "Back then you kept your husband. You married for better for worse. So, I knew from the very beginning that I have keep my husband. I could not let anybody take my husband." The husband who was looking at the other side of the coin stated: "When people ask: 'How come you have been with the same woman for that long?' My answer is: 'How can I train another wife for 60 years?'"

Here is important message for you as a person who is planning to marry or as a married partner. If you are planning to wed do realize that you have to train your partner. You have also to work hard to maintain your marriage. As a spouse do whatever you can to make your partner be fully convinced that you are his/her best friend? Do this when you are dealing with big and small things. Do realize that you have to train your partner. This must be done in love. We have been with my wife for forty-six years. And I should admit that there has been mutual training. We married when I was an Evangelist. Mary would not have liked to be a wife of a clergy. But through long life training, to day, she is not only a wife of an Archbishop, but she is also a clergy. And she does play both roles quite well. On the other hand, she has been training me for forty-six years. She particularly concentrated on working on me so as to improve my public image. This includes appearance and voice projection and how to deal with those we serve with honor and respect. She has indeed played a great role for me to be where I am.

Thus, as you work on your partner, you have to do everything in love. Remember what the Apostle Paul says: *Love is patient and kind; love is not jealousy and boastful, it is not arrogant and rude. Love does not insist on its own way, it is not irritable or restful; it does not rejoice on wrong but rejoices in right. Love… hopes all things and endures all things 1 Corinthians 13:4-5. True love comes from God. As the Apostle John has it "We love because he first loved us." This love is manifested in our love for each other and service to God and man.*

CHAPTER ELEVEN
LOVE FOR THE LORD AND THE MINISTRY

During a visit to the hospital, I enter a room which was charged with energy and humor. The patient was visited by her husband and seven members of the family. I was awed by positive feelings.

The patient had been married to the same husband for seventy years. Her husband was in a suit. He was looking like a bridegroom. The patient who was in bed was very receptive to pastoral care. She proudly told me that she has been married to the same man for 70 years and that she had 30 grandchildren. As she was talking her 66years old daughter entered the room. She greeted her: "Hi my little girl." "It is only my mom who calls me a little." She reported this to me. "Mom, I am not a little girl. I am a grown up and retired." The patient introduced her husband to me: "that is my younger husband." "What is that supposed to mean" I queried. "He is younger than me. He is only 91 years old. I am 94 years old. "What has kept you together for 70 years?" I asked. "We both love the Lord." Said the husband "And it is love for the Lord and the ministry which kept us together. I however valued my wife more that the ministry. She constituted 75% of my ministry." "I never pretended to be a pastor" added the wife. "If people came to me with pastoral questions, I told them "I am not your pastor." I referred them to my husband." This godly couple added: "fifty-five years which we ministered was the best time in our lives.

Lee and Jane have been married for 57 years and were

co-pastors for 50 years. They asserted that it was God and the ministry which gave them fruitful marriage. Also, whenever there was a conflict, they worked things through.

We need to tap in from this couple. Whether you are lay or pastor, when you faithfully minister together in the power of the Holy Spirit, the reward is the fellowship of the Holy Spirit. The Unitive Being gives you one mind and one heart. His love is like living water which flow in you and feel your life and ministry with vitality. We are rewarded by the Owner of the vineyard with the fruitful marriage. Our ministry becomes fruitful because we are in Him who said: "I am the vine; you are the branches. If a man remains in me and me in him, he will bear much fruit; apart from me you can do nothing." (John 15:5)

CHAPTER TWELVE
CHRIST AT THE CENTER

African American Couple who have been married for 40 years revealed their secret of success: "we put Jesus in the center. He is first in everything. Consequently, God has blessed us with our three children. One of our daughters is a counselor in the University, the other in a manager in the Mall and the other one is a Lawyer." The husband who is a Pastor added: We also minister God together. A white couple who have been married for 68 years contended that it was God and ministry which cemented their relationship: "We ministered together" the husband stated. "When there was a pastoral call, if I was not there she filled in for me." God has rewarded us by calling our son to the ministry."

Another Anglo couple who are co-pastors and have been married for 35 years revealed their secret of success: "we put God first, we are second, our children and everybody else are third. Whenever we get a new home, we kneel down and dedicate it to God. We have ministered here and as missionaries in Brazil where we started a medical clinic center. We use our money for the ministry and have always had a Bible study in our home."

Kim and Christ have been successfully married for 45 years. What is the secret of their success? Kim puts it this way: "Sometimes in our marriage I was tempted to walk away but the Lord Jesus brought me back to my husband. I didn't know the Lord when we were being married, I came to know

Him after marriage. When Jesus became our silence guest, we became more serious with our marriage vows. Unfortunately for the younger generation, marriage vows are empty words. For us they are powerful and binding; the younger generation marries to try out and if it doesn't work or if it is going to get tough, they break up.

John who has been married to Stacy for 50 years confessed. 'I was not good when we married, but when I was 34 years old, I committed my heart to Christ. After conversion I became devoted in reading the Bible and ministering to the homeless. And so, it was Christ in us and the ministry that builds up our relationship and gave us successfully marriage.

Roy who is a widower was married to the same wife for 60 years. He asserted: "the secret of our success was that we were both Christian and Baptist. So, the Love of Christ kept us together. We were also nurtured by our church. I loved my wife till death. I was with her when she was dying. After she died I felt her presence in the room, for a while. I believe God took her to a better place."

Pat and Joan have been in their second marriage for 24 years. They asserted that the secret for their second marriage is Christ "We both failed in our first marriage because we didn't have Christ. The second marriage is succeeding because we have put Christ in the center. We also knew each other since first grade. When we put Christ first, we succeed in marriage because "He is before all things, and in Him all things hold together." Colossians 1:17. In Christ, we don't just put up with each other, we enjoy each other.

CHAPTER THIRTEEN
PUTTING UP WITH EACH OTHER

Anglo couple who have been married for 67 years stated that the secret of their success is to put up with each other. The husband who is 6' 5" humbly stated: "she has put up with me. We are also proud of our son who has been married to same wife for 50 years. Another couple who have been married for 48 years also revealed the same secret. We put out with each other but we also enjoy each other. I really experienced joy, humor and positive feeling from these couples.

Putting up with each other is vital since humans are different personality types. Extrovert I spouse prefer countless friends while introverted (I) does not. For E things become clear as she talks; I prefer to think before he talks. E dominates the talk; while I control the silence. E enjoys energy expenditure, while I conserve the energy. E can move from party to party, this drains I.

There will also be conflicts if one is Thinker (T) while the other is Feeler (F). T is objective; F is subjective. T is firm-minded; F is fair-hearted. T put emphasis on justice; F is interested in being humane. T seem to be detached while F is involved. Sensor(S) has conflicting world view with Intuitive (N). S pays more attention to the present while (I) pays more attention to the future. This is a conflicting and compensation between my wife and me. When we are somewhere Mary is there a hundred per cent while I am there on fifty percent. Consequently, she remembers and episode which took place forty-five years ago with minute detail. Most of the time when she narrates the episode it is almost too detail for more. On the other hand, most of the episodes which I report to her don't have enough detail. She enjoys detail for the sake of detail while I prefer only the details that I can use. Positively she contributes immensely to our conversation. Furthermore, if one spouse is a Judger (J) and the other is Perceiver (P). J is decisive; P has "wait and see" attitude. J likes scheduling and deadlines while P like spontaneity and is irritated by deadline. The strong connecting thread between my wife and I is that we are both J. For more information read John Githiga, *Initiation and Pastoral Psychology*, the chapter on Division of Labor. The book is available at amazon.com.

CHAPTER FOURTEEN
HUMOR AND HARD WORK

The Anglo couple who have been married for 43 years maintained that humor and hard work has been the secret of their success. Asked why they have been together for so long, the husband who is a police officer and a clown said: "I took her to Wal-Mart in order to trade her in but no one who would take her." "See what I have to put up with", the wife responded. "But in the matter of fact both of us has worked hard on it." "We did this until the emergence of the women liberation which has been telling us that we are equal." "What you see is what is happening in political world". I commented. We have women in leadership. The former speaker of the House was a woman. Sarah Palin was John McCain's running mate. "But see what happening- economic crisis is." He jokingly blames it on women. "How do you relate to your wife as a married partner rather than as a police officer relates to a criminal?" I kidded." "I have handicapped her several times." Interestingly, the wife seemed to enjoy her husband's jokes while the husband was enjoying the seriousness of his wife. In this discussion, we learn a profound lesson about the success in marriage.

First, you have to expect your partner to evolve. Humans are influenced by the society in which they live. The movements such as civil rights, women liberation influence our ontology- awareness of self. Second, while humans were never gorilla or monkey, they have been evolving to either something better or worse. And in the process, there are elements which are emancipated. In matriarchal age the masculine component (animus) was suppressed; while in patriarchal age the feminine component (anima) was repressed. Our time is witnessing emancipation of both anima and animus. Thus, married partners should not only accept what they were and what they are but what they are becoming. This makes relationship both challenging and enjoyable as well. We need to face these changes with lightheartedness and with humor as this couple.

Another couple who had been married for 57 years claimed that hard work was the secret of their success. "When we were preparing for marriage some friends told us our marriage will not last because I am Hispanic and he is Anglo. They were wrong. He was a city boy and I was a country girl. I had to train him to work hard. We work hard in the farm and we still work." She is right, the husband confirmed. She is eighty-one and this week we were working on concrete and she lifted one hundred pounds of cement." This was incredible since when was 5' and possibly weigh 100Ib. This lovely couple informed me that they like doing manual work together. They watch TV together and that when their children were with them, they watched TV together. They now walk in Westgate Mall together regularly for exercise. The husband who is four years younger is the one who drives. "My husband wouldn't allow me to drive." The wife reported to me.

Interestingly, there is parallel between the couple and Mary and I. Mary was born in the city while I was born in the country side. We compensate each other by our different upbringing. We have always worked in the ministry. We start the day with devotions which included reading Daily Offices-

This entails reading concurrently two books from the Old Testament and two from the New Testament. We sing at least three songs and then pray for the global ministry. At St. Cyprian's international Church, she leads us in music and assist me in Holy Communion, while I preach and celebrate the Eucharist.

Additionally, we have division of labor at home. I pay the bills and do the book keeping, do the yard work, take out the garbage. She makes most of the decisions relating to Kitchen. She cooks; I serve. Together we wash the ditches. She does the laundry. And thus, by helping each other we have enjoyed living together for forty-six years.

And thus, we advise married partners to work together. "By love serve one another." Paul advises. Remembering that "For the Son of man did not come to be served, but to serve, and to give his life as a ransom for many." Mark 10: 45.

True friends are those who can cry together and laugh together.

CHAPTER FIFTEEN
FRIENDSHIP

Jack and Elena who have been married for 61 years firmly believe that friendship is the secret of their success. "We married when I was 18" said Jack "she was 17. We were great friends. We were friends then and have always been friends. We don't fight. But we discuss. When we were younger we used to have a heated discussion. Our children who knew that we were friends would intervene and say. 'Now the two friends are fighting!" and then we would respond "we are not fighting. We are discussing. We also know how to stop when the discussion become too hot. Basically, my wife touches my toe with her toe. When she does that, I immediately know that I must quit arguing. We also never go to bed in anger. Whenever we have a difference, we must deal with it before we go to bed. "

Mary and James who have been married for 48 years affirm that it was friendship which started from their childhood, which has kept them together. "We know each other since childhood. I was a girl next door. We have been friends ever since. We also believe in God and it is God who has held us together. The community of faith has also nurtured us. We go to church regularly. We also have a philosophy of life and death. We believe where are alive because there are people to see and the things to do. When our work is done the Lord will take us home.

Lisa and Bill have been married for 35 years. I found Liza in a surgery waiting room waiting for her husband who was having a bypass. She appeared drained. After comforting her, I asked her 'Where are you from?" I don't have "a where from" "What is that supposed to mean" I queried. "I have lived all over.' She responded. "I was born in Tokyo and we have moved everywhere. "It sounds that the whole world is your home. You look tired." "I am really tired and drained. This week I have to put my mother in law in the hospital and I have to wait for 38 hours. As soon as I went home my husband had chest pain and I have to rush him to the hospital." After praying with her we resumed our conversation. "How long have you been married?" "Forever" she responded. What is that supposed to mean. "I was married when I was 15 and my husband was 18. "What has kept you together" "He is the best man under the sun he was and still is my best friend. I cannot trade him for anything or anybody else. When we married people complained that I was a child. My mother in law couldn't even attend my wedding. But I forgive her and eventually she became my best friend and I, the best daughter in law. She has six sons who have married and divorced several times. But the baby girl has stayed married and I am the most cherished by father and mother in law. So, what has kept us together is God and friendship. "

Larry and Jane who had been married for 64 years stated that the secret of their success is:

"Not only that we are friends, we enjoy each other. We enjoy and love God and the church."

Friendship results to a good relationship. It is friends who make life good and enjoyable. As Helen Keller contended: "When I recollect the treasure of friendship that has been bestowed upon me, I withdraw all the charges against life. If much has been denied of me, much, very much, has been given me. So long as the memory of certain beloved friends lives in my heart, I shall say that life is good." When we are friends we give ourselves to each other a hundred percent.

CHAPTER SIXTEEN
A HUNDRED PER CENT DEAL

James and Sarah maintain that their secret is a 100% deal. She was 17 and I was 19 when we married. She used to sell ice cream. "And what won my heart was that my friends and I went to buy ice cream. She gave everybody one dip, but she gave me double dips. There and then I was convinced that she is a good girl and she will be my wife. After becoming friends for a while I snatched her from her parents" "This sound like old African way" I interjected. That is what I did. But we both learned that we don't have to give 50 % to each other but 100%. This has kept us together for 65 years.

Joy and David who have been married for 40 years maintain that their success is based on realization that it will never be 50 50. At time one partner has given 60% while the other is giving 40% and other time one partner gives 30% while the other is give 70%. I found lot of wisdom in this realization since one partner may be sick or depressed which will necessitated the other partner giving more of his/her time and energy.

As I was comforting the husband who was in the sickbed, the wife who had dementia, and was will dressed, communicated her love by holding my hand. The husband who was physically sick was the brain for his wife who kept on asking "how many children do we have?" "Three" Jack responded. I saw what they meant by being there for each other 100%. Real friendship implies acting in the interest of the other person. I like the way Leith Anderson puts it: "Biblical love is 'action in the best interest of the other person.' Ultimately it would be good to feel love and do love, but loving other is most about the doing. In other words, Christians love others even when we don't feel like it. Love is what we do." Christian married partners will strive to do good even in bad circumstances. They know that they will harvest what they have plants. They hid the word of God which advises: *Let us not become weary in doing good. For at the proper time we will reap a harvest if we do not give up. Therefore, as we have opportunity, let us do good to all people, especially to those who belong to the family of believers. (*Galatians 6:9-10.) And of course, we start with our spouses.

Traditionally the Africans trained boys and girls to be good to each other by valuing their sexuality by remaining virgins. This was true in African culture and Native American custom.

CHAPTER SEVENTEEN
A GIFT OF VIRGINITY

Joy, a Native American and a widow who was married to the same husband for 48 years asserted that Virginity was the secret of their success. "My parents who were Indians use to have ceaseless fight. When I was a little girl, I used to hind under the table as they fought. But my aunt taught me about the secret of success in marriage. She told me: 'the biggest gift you can give to your husband on the wedding day is your virginity.' I took her advice seriously. And so, virginity is what I gave to my bridegroom. Other things which cemented our marriage are our faith in God. We also gave each other freedom. He allowed me to stay at home, and I allowed him to go out to hunt, but I didn't allow him to take drugs or alcohol or to chase women. We loved each other and there was mutual respect.'

During a marriage seminar held in Nakuru, which we have mentioned, a single lady who is a lawyer is argued convincingly about the importance of virginity. She contended that chastity before marriage is the foundation of a successful marriage and that without this virtue is just like building the house without a foundation. By ignoring this virtue, I believe this is how fifty per cent of the marriages in the USA ends in divorce. The trend of free sex which started in 1960s has a devastating effect in marriage and family. For those who are not married we strongly advise them to value their sexuality by being virgin. This is not just a requirement for girls. It is also for boys. African tradition advocated virginity for both sexes.

In my community, after initiation, males and female, danced together and a boy was allowed to sleep in the same bed with his girlfriend and exercise platonic love and if a boy could try to penetrate, the girl would report him to the age group. And the boy was disciplined by the group by composing a song against him. Unfortunately, in Islamic world, it is only women who are expected to be virgins while male is as free as a he-goat to have sex with many girls. Ayaan Hirsi Ali, in *The Caged Virgin* writes: "when it concerns their sexuality, men in Islamic culture are seen as irresponsible, unpredictable, scary beasts who immediately lose all self-control upon seeing a woman." On the other hand, Muslim girls are often told that "a girl with a ruptured hymen is like a used object". And an object that is once used becomes permanently worthless. And of course, if she is raped by the he-goat she is condemned as adulterous and consequently she is flogged a hundred time. Christian men must value their sexuality as well as girls 'sexuality. Both sexes must exercise self-control till marriage.

Couples who were faithful to God and to each other before marriage tends to have mutual trust. When one partner goes way for business, the other has a feeling that if he was faithful he will be faithful as he was during the courtship. He had self-control then; he has self-control today.

It is also important that each partner protects the other. We live in a dangerous world, with pornographic movies and literature and drugs. Telecommunication superhighway come with centrifugal forces. The married partners should have a good sexual relationship. They need to heed St. Paul's advice: *"The husband should fulfil his marital duty to his wife, and likewise the wife to her husband. The wife's body does not belong to her alone but also to her husband. In the same way the husband's body does not belong to him alone, but also to his wife. Do not deprive each other except by mutual consent and for a time, so that you may devote yourself to prayer. Then come back together again so that Satan will not tempt you because of your lack of self-control* "(Corinthian 7:3)

CHAPTER EIGHTEEN
A GOOD SEXUAL RELATIONSHIP

While Joy contends that one of the secret of their success was to give her bridegroom a gift of virginity, a Laotian husband confirmed that good sex was one of the bases of their success. I interviewed George when he was visiting his wife who has suffering from cancer. He contended that success in marriage is not one thing. "A good marriage is like a good food which requires many ingredients which include relationship, having many things in common and good sex." He was right. A good number of failed marriages were resulted from poor sexual relationship which is, more often than not, a symptom of many problems. I was counseling a Native American couple, when I asked them about their sexual relations, the wife responded: "having a sex with him is a torture." Another parishioner who was a divorced American Indian, she never enjoyed sex with him because he used to look at his watch and say: "I give you five minutes to prepare yourself for sex." If the husband has to be like a he-goat to his wife, they will not have "a good sex." Sex will always be a torture to the wife which will affect all other areas of life.

Daniel Akin in *God and Sex* observe seven areas which need our careful thinking and *commitment*.

    1.   *Educationally*: study marriage and became a real student of it. Study the opposite sex and become an expert on them. Be a life time adventure. Study your spouse and get to know him/her. The author would add that no two women are exactly the same. Not only that they are unique individual but are also in the process of becoming. The saying: "no one crosses the same river twice" applies to your spouse.

2. Sexually: Take care of each other. Know the different between your needs and your wants. Exercise self- control. Resist outside temptation. Never bargain with sex. Don't become a marital prostitute who demands: "to play you must pay." This is a lose-lose proposition. Have mutual consent. I Corinthians 7:1-7). Don't expect your spouse to have the same appetite and desire that you have. While the husband may be starting lighting the fire, he should let the wife lead the way. When he is in, he has to exercise self-control.

3. Individually: Do not make a unilateral decision which affects your relationship. Do not depend primarily on your spouse for a sense of self-worth. Look for God to satisfy your spiritual needs.

When you make mistake say: "I am sorry, will you forgive me.?" Deal with your own sins first before dealing with your mate's.

4. Publicly: Keep confidential matters confidential. Never criticize your spouse in public or in in front of others. Guard the way you dress. Check your motives and your judgment.

5. Parentally: set up disciplinary policies jointly and stick on them. (Ephesians 6:1-4)

Don't argue about discipline in front of your children. Be loving and always restore fellowship after discipline. Discipline in a manner that is appropriate to the child's action and age.

6. Financially: Set up financial priority. Remember, no one is entitled to a superior status just because one earns the money to pay the rent and buy groceries. All who share in the labor to maintain the family ought to share in everything the family earns or produces.

7. **Relationally**: Take each other seriously but not too seriously. Nurture each other (Ephesians 5:29-30). Set up a problem-solving strategy. Be careful and courteous at all times. Treat your spouse as a good friend. Spend quality and quantity time with your spouse and family. Make room for intimacy and affection without pushing for sex. Treat each other as equals because you are equal. Be honest with each other; always speak the truth in love. (Ephesians 4:15.) Give you spouse practical and relational priority in all aspect of life. Be slow to anger, slow to speak and quick to listen. James 1:19. Do not let the sun go down in your anger (Ephesians 4:29). Never stop caring and pleasing your spouse (Philippians 2:2).

In addition, apply all the secrets which we have discussed. As married partners, remember sexuality is one of the most important things that the Creator has given to the creation. By sexuality we refer to vital spiritual energy which is demonstrated by hand-shaking, hugging, teasing, smiling and laughter. This energy gives us a loving, warm and cordial feeling toward each other. Sexuality is God-given and is our birth right. The creation story puts it this way: "God created man in his own image, in the image of God He created them, **male and female** He created them." The Holy Trinity ("Let Us") created them as male and female because he saw that "It was not good for a man to be alone." When he created, He look at what He has created:

"And behold, it was very good." Married partners ought to have God-attitude toward sexuality:

"Behold, it is very good." You should cherish it more than a farmer cherishes his farm.

CHAPTER NINETEEN
FARM AND CHILDREN

Glen and Wendy who have been married for 57 years maintained that their strong roots resulted from their farming and children. "All our energy was directed to children and farming. We thought and talked about and guided our children who stayed in the farm until they were mature adults. Influenced by our occupation, my two sons are in farming and cattle business. Our daughter has a degree in business and merchandising and runs her own business. Our two boys and two girls ply rodeo. They all followed our footsteps, and we really felt empty nest when they left." Of course, we cannot all be farmers. But we can learn from the farmer. James advises: *"Be patient, brothers until the Lord's coming. See how a farmer waits for the land to yield its valuable crops and how patient he is for autumn and spring rains. You too be patient and stand firm"* (James 5:7-8a).

If you are unmarried and the Lord guides to a city girl, don't hesitate to propose to her. While your farming life will bring something of great value in the relations; city partner will compensate what is lacking in your life. As mentioned above there is mutual training. My wife is a city girl. Recently we bought her a car which we named "city girl" I remember when I reported to my family who are farmers that I have proposed a girl from the city. The quick reaction was: Ah! Can a good girl come from the city? But the love I had for her was so great that not even an Angel could separate us. I was so surprised how she trained herself in farming. Today when it comes to farming

I tend to be in passenger seat. At her own initiative she bought the only a farm that we have. She manager and work on our back-yard garden. She has also trained me to be an urbanite. Most of our marriage life we have lived and worked in urban area. At one occasion the city girl acted as my hero at a very critical episode. This was a time when I was fired by a Bishop. We had worked with this bishop for five years. When we started ministering the congregation, there were very few people in the Church. But within five years not only that we had tripled the size of congregants, but we had started several programs and the stewardship had improved tremendously. So, on the last meeting with the bishop who has to tell us why we had to go, he told me that I had to go because of two things: African-ness and accent. I was devastated and almost speechless. Before we parted the City, Girl held Bishop by the shoulder and looked him direct at his face and said; "Bishop may I ask you a question?" "Yes Mary" He responded. "Are you a Christian?" "Yes I am." He responded with a heavy Southern accent. "If you are a Christian, be listening to good people not the bad people. Those people told you only what they thought you wanted to hear. Be a shepherd to your priest. It can be cold there." Not only that the City Girl had the last word, but she was also right. The issue was that the woman who accused the priest for accent and African-ness, wanted to have sex with the priest but the priest refused. When he refused she told him: "I will put you on the street." The street was the Bishop. After she had done this she was tortured by her conscious and called the priest "Father forgive me for lying to the bishop about you." "Could you pick up the phone and call the bishop and told him that you lied to him". The priest demanded. "Sorry, I don't have courage to do that." She responded. When the good people heard that their priest is being fired, one of them who was a professor visited with the Bishop and asked him why he had fired the priest. The bishop told her that it was not him but the Vestry (Church Council). She then confronted the council which informed her: "it is not us, it is the Bishop." So, the City Girl was right when she advised the Bishop "Be listening to good people not bad people."

Being the father of all nations, I strongly advise young people not only to break the barriers between farming and urban communities, but also between races and tribes. I have a blessing of having bishops and priests with intermarriages. These servants are bringing tremendous quality in the ministry. Bishop Steven, a Welsh, is married to Canadian. By being integrated they have an integrated Church with fifteen nations. Bishop Tom Brown, an Anglo married to a Spanish has an integrated congregation where Tom is a minority. Gordon and Mary Onyango in

Nakuru, Kenya, are from different community. The clergy conference which they organized in

July, 2014 had a diversity of ethnic groups. Of course, the conference was held in All Nations Church. I was surprised by the diversity and the spiritual gifts of the integrated community. Not only that they gave love offering but they also gave me a Kikuyu Bible. Bishop George and Jenny who take care of ANCCI farm are from different tribes. When we visited them in Zambia, we enjoyed their friendly confrontation. They had a blessing of seeing the both sides of the coin. At one occasion Jenny introduced a motion on how one must participate in his salvation. "When a baby is being born it must participate in pushing." She argued. "Let's dissect the story." George interjected. "The Bible says 'For by grace you have been saved, through faith –and this is not from your selves it is the gift of God-not by work, so that no one can boast (Ephesians 2:8-9). I then came to Jenny's aid by quoting Paul: "Continue to work on your own salvation with fear and trembling "Also James tells us "faith without work, is dead." After being with this lovely couple for seven days, Jenny posed another question to George. "George, if you go away for seven days, will you miss me?" After contemplating, George responded: "Home is home." "Does that mean you will miss me?" Jenny queried. "I don't say I will miss you, I said: 'home is home.' Interesting none of them was being offended. The lesson here for the married partners is that even if you are from the same community you don't have be swallowed by your partner. In both cases George and Jenny were dealing with a paradoxical truth. Most of the issues, in the deepest sense are paradoxical. This discussion was followed by a very interesting story about the birth of little George, whom we declared as All Nations baby during the gathering of Nations in Thika. George Jr was the only baby who attended the event and Mama Mary gave him a shirt with images of children of all colors. Jenny told us how he was born. "He delayed for one month and the doctor told me that I will have him through surgery. I then talked to God and said: 'God, if you are alive, and if you are my Father, and if you want me to be bishop's wife, let me have this baby on a particular day and time without surgery." So, she gave God a deadline.

And amazingly, George Jr was born an hour before the deadline and without surgery. And few months later, Father George was consecrated a bishop. So, Jenny knew what she was talking about when she said that a baby must participate in pushing. Our arguments here is that intermarried couples have additional benefit of seeing the other side of the coin and are being used by God to fight tribalism and racism.

KTN presented a story of intermarriage between Sarika Patel an Asian girl and Timothy Kamala a Bukusu young man who was a family employee. The two lovers have to deal with racial, cast and color barriers. The Asian girl had to defied parents' rules and racial taboo, new Timothy for four years. She is the one who proposed Timothy who is described as shy and a man of few words. In the interview Sarika was asked whether it is true that her parents have confiscated her car and closed her bank account. She confessed that she doesn't either have an account or a car and that she doesn't care about money- "I see money as just papers and what matters is love. Timothy was asked whether he expected to get dowry from the parents of Sareka as it is Asians custom. He responded in Swahili: *Sina haja ya pesa za wahidi, nilicho haja nacho ni mapezi* . I don't care about the Asian money all that I care about is the love between me and Sareka. She however, became a star in this community and she is dearly loved by Timothy's parents and the Wembuye community.

I believe intermarried couples will play a vital role of breaking the wall of hostility between races and tribes and social strata.

If you are city person and God guides you to a farming community, do realized that your partner will compensate what is lacking in your community. If God guides you to another race or community; go for it. But you must be ready to study the family tree and the cultures of your partner. Respect your partner's culture and when there is a disagreement, you need to disagree agreeably. Equip yourself with Christian ethics which Paul refers as a fruit of Spirit which is *"love, joy, peace, patience, kindness, goodness, faithfulness, gentleness and self-control."* How do you acquire this fruit? The answer is closer to you than your nose is close to your mouth. Right now, as you are reading this page, listen to what the Prince of Peace says: *"Hear Am! I stand at the door and nock, if anyone hears my voice and open the door, I will come in and eat with him, and he with me"* (Revelation 3:20).

Intermarriage couples need to realize that even the partners from the same culture differ. There is, therefore no greener pasture on the other side of the fence. Do also realize that sex urges are not always on the same level. Therefore, there is a time one has chase his/her partner in love.

CHAPTER TWENTY
CHASE HIM/HER

I was tickled by the couple who have been married for 80 years. They were at their 90s. I interviewed them in a restaurant. The wife had hearing loss. The husband who had a strong sense humors revealed their secret: "She chances me all over the house. Second, she is humorous." I believe in a good marriage there need to be time of chasing each other. It is a typical thing when one is sexually high, the other is low. The one who is high need to "ask for her things". After all, your man belongs to you. It is better to chase him than to complain. It is most likely that one partner was chasing the other in the morning of their life but is now chased in the afternoon or twilight of their life. You need to heed words of wisdom from the Apostle Paul: *"The husband must fulfill marital duty to his wife, and likewise the wife to her husband. The wife's body does not belong to her alone, but also to her husband. In the same way the husband's body does not belong to him alone but also to his wife. Do not deprive each other except for mutual consent and for a time, so that you may devote yourself in prayer"* (I Corinthian 7:3-5).

As stated above it is better for one who is high to claim his/her things with love and a sense of humor rather than having an extra marital affair or contemplating on divorce or punishing the other partner in some other ways. If a 98-year-old can still chase her husband, how about you? Don't you have self-determination?

CHAPTER TWENTY-ONE
DETERMINATION

As I was going the restroom, I found a woman standing at the door of the men's room. As I draw near to her she told me that she was waiting for her husband, but "there is more than one spot. You go in." upon

entering, I found the man standing before the wheel chair relieving himself. When I was done, I found the lady was still waiting for her husband. How long have you been together"? Fifty-two years." "Fifty-two years! What has held you together?" I queried. "Determination. When we married we were fully convinced that marriage is forever." From the observation, I learned that the couple was there to be together and help each other to the end. Most of the couples I interviewed indicated that their successes were not based on feeling but have made a firm decision that they will be together for better for worse. They have fully resolved to do what is right. Their decision was not based on feeling. The woman we have mentioned above did not care what men will think by seeing her standing on men's comfort room. They had firm and fixed intention to be together to the very end. They had perseverance and persistency and tenacity.

Archbishop Manasess Kuria who is my role model was surprised to learn that he stayed married to his wife even after she was called to glory. He once said to me: "I used to tell the couples when I was ceremonizing their marriage that they will be together until they are parted by death, but I still feel marriage to my wife even when she has gone to be with the Lord.

Couples with great determination have strong belief that they can. President Baraka Obama favorite words were "Yes we can." Henry Ford made a great statement in this regard: "The man who thinks he can and the man who thinks he can't are both right. Which one are you?" Those who succeed in marriage are those who believe that they can. For them marriage is not temporary; it is for life. And for that reason, even when the journey becomes hazy they never give up. Winston Churchill famous statement was: "Never give in. Never give in. Never, never, never, never- in nothing, great or small, large or pretty- never give in, except to the conviction of honor and good sense." Thus, couples who are determine to stay to gather for life are ready not only to give fifty percent, but also a hundred percent. They are for each other for better for worse, for richer, for poorer.

This is a determination of doing what is right. As we have recorded, some believe they have to give a fifty per cent while others were convinced that they have to give a hundred percent. For better for worse, for richer, for poorer. When we have determination, we reach out to each other. We hold each other's hands to the end.

CHAPTER TWENTY-TWO
HOLDING EACH OTHERS HAND

The partners who hold each other hands in public are likely do the same mind in private. Joe and Jane are in the Nursing home have been married for 60 years. Jane was hard of hearing but Joe was the spoke's person. I was sitting at the living room of the home while Joe was wheeling his wife. When they came to me, we had a short talk, and then I asked them about the secret of their success:

"I cannot tell you. It is our secret." At the meantime they were holding each other hands tenderly. "Your secret may help the younger generation." I responded. "The young generation does not think that the old people have anything to offer." But I come from a society which respect the senior citizen so your secret will be useful to me." "I am sorry; I will not tell you our secret." He then wheeled his wife back to their room. However, their body language spoke louder than the words. I remember an episode which takes place at Githiga Memorial Church at Ichichi where I was born. We were attending my mother's memorial service. As we were coming from the church, I held wife's hand to save her from tripping on stair way. I was reprimanded by the Diocesan Bishop (even though I was Archbishop) for holding my wife's hand to save her from tripping on the stairs. The Diocesan (who Freud would refer to as "His majesty the boy) complained "We do not hold our wives' hands in Africa." We must set ourselves free from conditioning taboos. If my wife and I are one body, why should I be ashamed to hold her hand in public? Doesn't the Bible tell us "Husbands, love your wives, just as Christ love the church and gave himself for her?" If she is my body, why should I be ashamed to hold her hand in public? Not only that we have right to hold hands in public, we should also complement each other in public. I was a Hospital Chaplain, I was very much impressed by a husband who met me at the door as I was visiting his sick wife. "She is the most beautiful woman that I have ever seen. She was beautiful when we were dating, she is still beautiful. Let us give her time to finish making a call which she is making and then you will visit her." When I entered, I could see the beauty in her eyes as I was giving her pastoral care. I was very proud of this man for the love and respect he has for his wife. We should also remember that the Lord holds us in the palm of his hand. Holding each other's hand is a nonverbal communication of love.

CHAPTER TWENTY-THREE
COMMUNICATION

Briggs and Stacy who have been married for fourteen years believe that communication is the key to success in marital relationship. There is a Kikuyu love song which states: Communication fosters love; silence fosters hate. There are many marriages which grow cold because of lack of communication. In this relationship, one of the partners applies passive aggression whereby he doesn't talk to the other partners. When, however he is with other people he talks and laughs with friends even the strangers but refrains from talking to his mate. This foster hate and strife in marriage.

C G Jung, the father of psychoanalysis, contends that communication is the key to the therapy: he holds that communication is therapy and therapy is communication.

There is healthy communication and unhealthy communication. The first is the key to success and latter leads to unhealthy marriage relationship. This becomes evident particularly in conflict management. How the conflict is dealt with can bring partners together or tear them apart.

To maintain a good relationship, the partners need to listen to each other carefully rather than paying more attention to what one is going to say next. While it might be difficulty try to listen what your partner is saying you. You can check whether you have heard it correctly by reflecting back what she has said. When you understand her better, she will also try to listen.

Stay focused on the issue at hand. Don't bring past

related issues. This will only complicate the issue at hand and make it difficult to find the solution.

Be gentle and patient when criticism come with emotional. If one partner is a feeling type while the other is a thinking type, the latter is surprised by the former. In a marriage seminar we had in Germany, a lady who must be a thinking type had this to say: "I wish God had created humans without feeling." The feelers can express their views with strong feeling and emotion and this can be devastating to the thinking type. The thinking type can, however, listen with calmness. Better still listen to each other empathetically. Avoid dwelling on the past. Each one ought to own what is theirs. It takes a strong person to accept when one is wrong and to ask for forgiveness. It also takes a strong person to forgive and to let it go. Remember humans are imperfect. To error is human; to forgive is divine. And thus, we need to go beyond tolerance to love. By love talk to each other and serve one another.

Briggs and Stacy who have hosted me several times in Phoenix Arizona, are very good at talking to each other. One will tell his partner what is in his/her mind. They also communicate love. Most of the time, they parted with the words: "I love you." It is very important that the partners communicate love. During my recent overseas mission, I observed the same pattern of communication between Bishop Evan and Mikah, Archbishop William and Helen and Canon Habel and Mary. When on the trip, Steven called Mikah at least three times to let her know where we were and to consult her about something. He referred to her as honey or darling. William who had to take me to the mission, called Helen several times. Habel who accompanied me for two weeks and slept with me in the same room called Mary twice a night- 1.00am to remind her to awake their granddaughter for bathroom and at 4.30 to check whether she has taken hot water so as to have morning devotion. I was surprised to note that whenever he called Mary was up. The main reason for call was fellowship which is based in Christ and the Word of God.

Thus, we need to communicate both *agape* and *Eros*. For Christians this will be both Eros and agape. Agape is the love that gives and receives. Saint Paul's defines agape as: "Love is patient, love is kind. It does not envy, it does not boast, it is not proud. It is not rude, it is not self- seeking, it is not easily angered, and it keeps no records of wrongs. Love does not delight in evil but rejoices with truth. It always protects, always trusts, always hopes, always persevere" (I Corinthians 13:4-7).

When agape is coupled with Eros, the partners will have warm positive attitudes toward each other. They will hold hands. They will hug. They will kiss and enjoy their sexuality. Lovers do not have unrealistic expectations of each other. They never use silence as a weapon.

CHAPTER TWENTY-FOUR
WE DON'T USE SILENCE AS A WEAPON

Michael and Ruth are Anglos have been married for 40 years and are doctors of theology. Ruth who was eager to reveal the secret stated: "we don't use silence as a weapon. Whenever there is anything between us, we talk it over and we don't go to bed with anger. Michael has a good sense of humors and we also laugh a lot." This is in keeping with the Kikuyu love song which we have mentioned earlier: Communication fosters love. Silence fosters hatred.

As we have mentioned there are married partners particularly the introvert who employs silence to punish their partners. They talk and laugh with their friends but when their spouses come in they keep silence. They normally do this to the partner who an extrovert. This behavior is devastating and must be resisted in marriage. The person, who is using this deadly weapon, may even talk with his children but will not talk to their father or their mother. Silence as a weapon is very much like suicide bomb. It destroys bother user and the targeted person; the Palmist put it this way: *"When I kept silence, my bones wasted way through my groaning all day long...My strength was sapped as in the heat of the summer"* (Psalm 32:3-4). Thus, silence brings pain to both partners. The Psalmist testifies how he used silence but, in the end, it became toxic to him: "But when I was silent and still, not even saying anything good, my anguish increased" (Psalm 39:2).

If your partner is using silence as a weapon, find out

whether you are using words as a weapon.

And so instead of trying to win the argument, look for solution that meet everybody's needs. Try not to get your wants at the expenses of the other.

If the situation is not getting any better you need to ask for help. Visit your pastor or bishop for pastoral counseling. You can also visit a marriage counselor. Remember there are three Keys to success in all relationships: Forgiving, giving and thanksgiving. Do realize that none of you is perfect.

CHAPTER TWENTY-FIVE
NOT PERFECT BUT TENACIOUS

Couples (who were sick but with winsome smiles who have been married for 52 years and were at the late eighty's) summarized their secret with four words "Not perfect and tenacity." The husband said both had "I am not perfect and she is not perfect" attitude. I didn't expect her to be perfect and she didn't expect me to be perfect. This is one of the best attitudes toward one another. When one partner is perfectionist, she become too critical of the other partner and the children. A story is told of a wife who is a perfectionist. She always wants the house to immaculate clean. Not only that she expected dishes to be washed, but they must be arranged in a particular way. She was such a perfectionist that her children told her: "Even heaven will not be clean enough for our mom. "

The above-mentioned couple added something in the philosophy of life: Tenacity. The wife stated: "We had steadfastness in whatever we decided to do." The husband claimed that he was a slow learner but so disciplined that he was able to earn a Master's Degree in Education and did some doctoral program and was a successive teacher. "Not perfect" attitude entail, accepting that part of our partner which is unstructured. In *Initiation and Pastoral Psychology, we* have a chapter on *Mararanja*. The unstructured sphere of the psyche, we argue that a deep relationship is not reached until this realm is embraced and accepted. While this realm is a part of our personality, it tends to express itself when we are going through the rite of passage- moving from one place to another, from one developmental stage to another and from one social status to another. We have therefore to be magnanimous with our spouse. We have been patient with one another.

It is however vital that we be persistent in doing good and those things that build up. I am always astonished with some of the qualities that Mary has, nurturing and devotion to God.

Living in the same church compound I perceived this quality when she was ten-year-old. Whenever I visit her godparent, I will find her taking care of a sickly godfather. She fed him. She regularly attended Morning Prayer. She has shown the same commitment for the last 45 years that we have been together. She has persistently taken care of the elderly and terminally ill. This year she was awarded certificate of appreciation for eleven-year pastoral ministry to the hospice. She does this whether she is well or sick.

A marriage relationship requires persistence. House chores must be shared all the time. And whatever each partner is doing, he must be persistent. As Paul put it "by love, serve one another". To succeed in marriage, we must love and serve one another. Lack of love leads to failure.

CHAPTER TWENTY-SIX
OUR OPEN SECRET

Finally, I would like to share the secrets of our fruitful marriage. When we were in courtship, we adopted as our motto Saint Paul's words "I can do all things in Christ who strengthens me." As we were facing some challenges, the Holy Spirit encouraged us with this word. As with our Native American who had to give his partner a gift of virginity, Mary and I had to do the same. All our dates were held in the city park in open and during the day. After marriage we adopted Psalm 23 which we memorized and learned to sing by heart. We experienced our Loving Father as our Shepherd, who leads us in green pastures and besides the quiet waters. We also believed that he will restore our souls when where are beaten up by the challenges of life and ministry. We strongly believed that it is important to be faithful to each other and to God and that the Great Shepherd will guides us to the path of righteousness. The Lord of host assured us that He will not remove the shadows of the Valley of death, but strongly believed that He will guide us through these shadows. During our long life of ministry, we had faced the shadow of death in terms of physical sickness, psychological and economic tribulation and have come out stronger and more purged. We have been surprised by the Risen Lord with a banquet in the presence of our foes. He indeed gave us so many good things which we do not deserve. And we are fully convinced that goodness and mercy will follow us all the days of our lives and we will dwell in the house of the Lord forever.

Immediately after our wedding, we started reading the Gospel of John. And eventually we formed a habit of reading one book of the Bible. Then we formed a small Bible study group and we have been doing this for forty-four years.

When I was consecrated a Bishop in 2006, we started using Day Office (for more information visit www.dailyoffice.org). Daily office is an ancient way of praying which has been used by monasteries, churches and private homes for two thousand years. Bible readings include two reading from the OT and two from NT. The OT must include Psalms while NT must include the Gospel. As the body requires all nutrients to be healthy, our souls required nutrients from the Old Testament and the New Testament. We have learned that the NT is hidden in the OT and the OT is revealed in the new. The Psalmist seems to be with us when where are going through tribulation as well as the time of joy. In the Gospel we hear the voice of our Master. By using Daily office, we go through the whole Bible every two years. It also connects us with the Universal church since most denominations such Roman Catholic, Anglican, Methodist, Presbyterian, and the Disciples use daily office for their daily devotion. Since we started using Daily Office, Mary and I are more spiritually nourished.

We start devotions in our bedroom by singing at list three songs. We sing in Kikuyu, Swahili and

English. We then pray: *Open my eyes that I may see wonderful things in your law (*Psalm 118:18) After reading and meditating on the readings we pray for Christians of All Nations, our children and extended family, the Government, and those who are suffering in various ways.

This pattern of devotion has strengthened our life and has made our ministry more fruitful and has helped us to meet the challenges of life and has enabled us to "let the scriptures dwell in you richly".

We do encourage married partners to form this discipline. We promise that this will enrich your life and make it more fruitful. You can get Daily Office from www.satucket.com or the above-mentioned website. Daily Office is one of the cures of the causes of failure in Marriage.

CHAPTER TWENTY-SEVEN
PLANT THE SEED OF THE GOSPEL
GOLDEN WEDDING ANNIVERSARY

Mary and I are awed by the way God have been with us for fifty years. The words which guided us when we were in courtship were: "I can do all things through Christ who strengthens me." We also owned Psalm 23 "The Lord is my shepherd; I shall not be in want." We memorized this Psalm and we like singing it during our morning devotion. We have been dumfounded by the power of the Good Shepherd. As he promises: "No one can snitch them out of my hands". Satan has tried many times and has not succeeded. He works overtime particularly when we are preparing and taking off for missions December 16, 2018 and when we are planning the seed of the Gospel. Yet in spite of Satan's schemes, we are more than conquerors.

When we were celebrating our Golden wedding anniversary on December 16, 2018, we were amazed to learn that one of the reasons that God kept us together is being in Christ and bearing fruit. Our loving Savior also promised that if we remain in him, we will bear fruits and that the Father prunes the branches which don't bear fruits. In the last 50 years, God has terminated the relationships which would hinder us from bearing fruits. Christ do not command us to impossible but to let the Holy Spirit fill every fiber of our being. We then bear the fruits of the Spirit is love, joy ,peace, patience, kindness, goodness, faithfulness, gentleness and self-control. Galatian 5:22

We were so surprised by what we saw and experienced in our missions to Kenya in 2018. we were dumfounded by witnessing the growth of the seeds which we planted many years ago. The Golden anniversary included the great events which took place many years ago. Being commissioned as Church Army captain in 1964, the Captain of the first Nakuru Company of Boys and Girls Brigade(started by Presbyterian and Anglican Church), ordained Deacon in 1974; ordained priest in 1975 , and establishing the first KAMA (Kenya Anglican Men Association) in 1985. Surprisingly, today there are brigade companies in Anglican, Presbyterian and Methodist churches in Kenya. There are also KAMA in most Anglican Churches in Kenya. Startlingly, during our recent mission to Kenya, we attended 20th anniversary of Thika Diocese, the ceremony started with Boys and Girls Brigade parade. All the clergy paraded in brigade uninform with Bishop Julius the Chaplain. In 1964 when we started the first company in Kenya, we never imagined that anything of this magnitude, will occur. We were also amazed by the event which was organize by KAMA for mentoring a male child. The event was attended by males ranging from 5 to 76 years old focusing on training boys how to be men. They slaughter three goats and were taught how to prepare the meat. I never expected to see this in my life time. All the glory to God.

We got frenetic favor at All Saint Cathedral Nairobi at their thanking service. We were greeted by the Provost with: "I am the recipient of Githiga award- This is given to a student who excel on Practical Theology which Gideon and I taught at St. Paul University. St Nicholas, which was birth by St Nicholas children Home, Nakuru, sang: "plant the seed." We felt affirmed and encouraged to be starters. We also launched our book: *FROM VICTORY TO VICTORY* and were commissioned by the Archbishop of Kenya as missionaries to the Global Village.

Additionally, we experienced amazing grace in the Diocese of Mount Kenya Central where we stayed in the home of Bishop Timothy and Mrs. Gichere for three days. They accorded us wonderful hospitality. We ministered about 600 clergy and their spouses, 300 lay readers and their wives and three high schools. At Kahuhia Girls (where our daughter attended for 2 years, we were given golden anniversary cake with the students putting the cake in our mouth. What a blessing. We were surprised to find ourselves with students at Muguru high school where I attended Primary Top school in 1955-56 and was a warded a gift for Character. We talked to student about Christ and Character using the motto of Booker T Washington: "Character is power." We asked the student to repeat these words several time. Interesting, it was the Head teacher of this school, Bernard Mwangi, who planted the seed of the of the Gospel in me. I was seeing the radiant of God in him and made a song: "I will be saved." We had a blessing of visiting his grave. On the third day, we woke up 5.30 am so as to minister to St. James at 7am. God gave us a theme: Rejoice in the Lord always. To our surprise, the song they sung was "the joy of the Lord is my strength and Mary taught them: "Rejoice in the Lord always."

Furthermore, we had a blessing of ministering Nakuru Diocese, our canonical diocese, for three days. We minister about 500 clergy and their spouses staying in Imani center, at executive suit. We also enjoyed family reunion. We are most grateful to Bishop Dr Joseph and Mary Muchai for their love and hospitality.

Another wonder took place at Christ healing church where Patriarch was led to the church by a motor cade of eight motor cycles. We commissioned and ordained ministers and had Spirit filled service. we praise God for the ministry of Bishop John Njeru who brings together interdenominational and internationals pastors and Bishop. Bishop John prayed that God may give us long life that we may continue ministering together. Interestingly Bishop John testified that he prayed God for 11 years that God give may him a Spiritual father. The prayer was answered through Dr. Peter Mwiti who was my student at St. Paul's University, Kenya. Since we have so many children in every continent, it is difficult for us to accept all invitations. To be able to visit Bishop John, he wrote to us several times requesting us to visit him. When he found that we are not scheduling the visit, He cried out like a baby: "Oh,oh,oh, oh, oh Mom! I need to be breastfed!" His cry got our attention and we had to plan a visit to Embu.

We also launched ANCCI Institute which aims at spiritual, cultural and economic transformations. The practical action by institute was donation a pig in Embu, and three sheep to three families with an agreement that when they produce kids and piglets, the recipient will donate a female pig and a sheep to another family. The institute also established a theological center in Thika. All glory to the Great Provider

The main point in this chapter is that if we abide in

Christ, God will richly bless our marriage
And we will bear much fruits.

CHAPTER TWENTY-EIGHT
NURTURE YOUR BEST SELF

In addition to being in Christ we need to nurture our best self by developing **five virtues: 1. Vision-** which is ability to see what others do not see. **Courage-** The ability to act despise fear. **Creativity-** the ability to think outside the box. **Self-confidence-** The ability to withstand criticisms. **Self-control-** The ability to delay gratification.

How do the married couples get vision? In the case of Mary and I, we are given vision when we are reading the word of God and praying in Spirit. As Our loving Savior told the Samaritan woman: "God is the Spirit and his worshipers must worship him in Spirit and in truth. As Joel prophesied: "In the last days, God says, I will pour out my Spirit in all people, your sons and daughters will **prophesy**, your young men shall see **visions,** and your old men will dream **dreams**." Acts 2:17. This is all about visions. Prophecy in seeing a vision about God' will for his people and prediction of the future. The vision may come in a dream at night when we are sleeping or even during the day when we are awake.

My vision for Mary was a gradual process starting when she was 12-year-old when she read Isiah 5:1-8 in the family service at St. John's church, Nakuru Kenya. We were also the only teen who attended early morning prayer which was held from Monday to Friday. we taught children service and attend church youth meeting and youth camp where we were taught about friendship between boys and girls. we met at the home of her God parents who lived in the church compound. She was giving her sick godfather hospice care. As noted above we started the first Nakuru Boys' and Girl's together where I was the Captain and she was an Officer of Girls Brigade. I started being attracted too her because of her commitment to God and the ministry. She was also developing feeling for me. She shared with me how they played a game with other girls about the first name of a young man with a vision that if she has the same number of the letters in first name, that man is likely to be your future husband. So, John and Mary happened to have the same number. But she was also looking for the character and the commitment to God and Ministry. so eventually we were spiritually bonding and I had to propose her in the presence of her godmother. She did not say yes or no. But we started dates. having trained by Church Army to never let a young woman come alone to your house, we never had date in my house which was located at church compound. all our dates were held at the city park. we strongly believed that the best gift we will give to each other at our wedding was our virginity.

It is said that God does not give a vision without provision, but there is always a problem between a vision and provision. So, after dating, I reported to the priest about our friendship. Being an evangelist who was sharing the same pulpit with the priest who was jealousy of me; when I reported to the priest, without giving me a single word of advice, he reported me to our missionary Bishop, that I was dating immature girl(Mary is small in size-5' 2" - but superior in character). When the Bishop go the information, he quickly transfers me a hundred mile away from Mary. as I later learned from his missionery friends, he did this so that our love may grow cold. However, our love for each other did not grow cold.

Our big challenge was that the bishop went for four months leave to Australia and Mary and I were left hanging in the air. To my great surprise, Mary's family was very supportive. My 5 years old brother in low, George said: " If they have evicted Captain John, we are going to build him a house at our backyard." May father in law comforted me with word: "When someone is playing the game, the spectators will criticize him. So do not lose heart.

When the bishop returned, I visited him. To my greatest surprise, he consented. I then asked him to be our celebrant. He agreed. I ask him to give us the date of the celebration. To my utter surprise, he said: "Mary will give us the date." I then joyfully went and asked her the best date. She gave us the date which was December 7, 1958. The bishop consented to the date.

We were amazed by God's provision for dowry, and wedding reception and honey moon. When my team visited my inlays to bargain the dowry. My first advocate was my mother in law. she said: "before you decide how much you are doing to ask. Remember that Mary and John will need food after the wedding." My father in law responded: "all what I need is a pair of shoes." Then my team ask them to give a consent note. I was give consent even before I had bought a pair of shoes to my father in law. When we were planning for wedding reception, the team made so economical that we spent Kenya shillings 270. which was my salary. The wedding cake was provided by a

British missionary, the bridal driver was bishop's secretary who was a British. For our honey moon we were hosted by a Scottish Presbyterian missionary. He left us in his mansion with a cook who not only provided us with dinner, but also bed room coffee. We were give lot of gifts=money and utensils. And we started our live together with enough provision.

The message here for the married partners and those who are planning to marry is that you should not run way from challenges. As the Kikuyu proverb puts it: Blessing are beyond the obstacle."(Munyaka bere ya kahinga). Remember what Joseph went through after his dream-Being thrown to the ditch by his brothers and sold as a slave and thrown to prison by Potiphar's wife. So, you need to see challengers as stepping stone, not as obstacle.

CHAPTER TWENTY-NINE
CAUSES OF FAILURE IN MARRIAGE

In the following pages we are going to discuss the causes of failure in marriage and are going to draw from numerous marriage seminars I held in Kenya and my observation of failed marriages in the USA. In the marriage seminars in Kenya with the groups ranging from 20 to 700, I posed a question a question: "What spoils the relationship between a husband and wife?" The following were identified as the course of problems

1. *Lack of premarital counseling.*

Most young people enter into marriage without any counseling. The only information they have is what they get from their peer and the media. It has to be born in mind that marriage is one of the most complex institutions which has great impact on an individual. Your marriage partner constitutes the largest portion of your environment.

She is the first person to see in the morning and the last person to see at night. She /he will call you more than any other person. For this reason, premarital counseling is vital.

I do believe the one of the secrets of fruitful marriage between Mary and I is the counseling which we got from our pastor and his wife and our best man and best maid.

Moreover, the parish organized youth camps. It included the teaching on friendship between boys and girls. The teaching included "dos" and "don't s". We were taught how to value our sexuality and that the wedding cake should wait until the wedding day. That is, as the Native American was advised by her aunt, the best thing you can give to your partner is your virginity.

The Book of Common Prayer gives a good advice in this regard: "The union of husband and wife in heart, body, and mind is intended by God for their mutual joy; for the help and comfort given one another in prosperity and adversity, and, when it is God's will, for the procreation of children and their nurture in the knowledge and love of God, for the procreation of children and their nurture in the knowledge and love of the Lord. Therefore, marriage is not to be entered into unadvisedly or lightly, but reverently, deliberately and in accordance with the purpose for which it was instituted by God."

2. Cohabitation

Cohabit are basically self-centered and narcissistic. Their motive is "let's try and see whether it will work. My partner must prove himself/herself first. I must first eat the wedding cake." These partners are unethical and amoral. They defy customary law and Christian ethics. And this is why 99% the marriages which start with cohabitation end in divorce. During the marriage seminar we had in Nakuru, a single lady who is a lawyer argued convincingly that one of the causes of failure of the marriages today is premarital sexual intercourse. Most participants agreed with her. If you are unmarried, as it was with the Native American quoted before, the best gift you can give to your married partner is virginity. This applies to bother young men and women

3. Bad company

The Kikuyu has a saying: He who accompanies a bad

person becomes as bad as his companion (muchera *na mukundu a kundukaga ta guo*) If one partner or both are associating with persons who are taking drugs or alcohol or persons with divorce experience, this results in negative effect on their marriage.

4. Separation.

If one partner lives in the city while the other partner is in the countryside or if they live in a different country; they eventually grow a part and their marriage will end in separation. Living separately is against the will of the Creator. The creation story puts it this way: *"The Lord God said, "'it is not good for a man to be alone. I will make him a helper suitable for him.... So, the Lord God caused a man to fall into a deep sleep, and while he was asleep, he took one of the man's ribs and close up the place with flesh. Then the Lord made the woman from the rib he had taken out of the man, and he brought her to the man...For this reason man will leave his mother and father and be united to his wife, and they will become one flesh"* (Genesis 2:18-24). So how can the two who are one flesh live apart?

5. *Interferences- in-laws*.

As mentioned above the Bible make it clear that it is God's will for the man to leave his father and mother and cleave to his wife. Marriage is strained if one of the partners does not leave and cleave. It is even worse when the partners live in under the same roof in the same homestead with the parents. In marriage seminar which we had in California a man who sat with his wife asked: "Could you advise me on how wrestle with two bulls?" "Who are the bulls?" I asked. "My wife and my mother." Interestingly, the wife who sat with her husband didn't deny that she is one of the bulls that the man has to wrestle with. The husband's mother, a Kenyan, has moved to America so as to take care of the children. But being matriarch, she tries to assume the leadership, while the wife who is also a matriarch was unwilling to relinquish the leadership to her mother in law. The remedy to this marriage is leaving and cleaving. While the man has to honor his mother, he has to make a tough choice. While he has to support his mother, he has to cleave to his wife. For more information about this subject read my work:

Initiation and Pastoral Psychology.
6. Weak Spirituality.

Another secret of failure in marriage is weak spirituality. As we have seen from the couple whom I interviewed, most of them asserted that their good relationship with God was their secret of success. Partners who are not godly, often come to a marriage relationship with expectations that God and God alone can meet. They are very much like the Samaritan woman who hopped from one man to another. She had had five husbands and Jesus revealed to her that even her present husband is not actually her husband. Marriage without God lacks the fruits of the Spirit which is: *love, peace, joy, patience, kindness, goodness, faithfulness and self- control (Galatians 5:22).*
7. Poor Division of Labor

One of the secrets of failure in marriage is poor division of labor. In this case one partner is overworked while the other partner is a parasite. A large number of the people I interviewed about the secret of successes claimed that their successes were due to hard work of both of them. When I asked Jack about their secret he summarized his answer with two words: "Hard Work." A Mexican husband told me that the secret of their success was due to hard work. He said: "I have little time for watching TV. I had to do two jobs so as to give adequate support to my family."

As loving partners, you have to share house chores. You must know exactly who the book keeper is. Who prepares for the filing of taxes? Who is in charge of cooking, serving, washing the dishes, taking out the garbage, making the bed? As was with traditional kikuyu division of labor, there were jobs which were performed by both sexes. Other jobs were done by men while others were performed by women. See my: *Initiation and Pastoral Psychology.* As St. Paul advises: "By love serves one another." "He who does not work let him not eat."

The secret of success in division of labor is letting the Spirit of God fill every fiber of our beings.

So, when the married partners put God in their lives, they will enjoy work and enjoy themselves. Interestingly work preceded the fall. Man was created for work. As the creation story puts it: "The Lord God took the man and put him in the Garden of Eden to work and take care of it" (Genesis 2:15). Not only that we were created for work, but the Creator within us gives us will and energy for doing what we are supposed to do for the family. This is what he says: *"Do you not know? Have you not heard? The Lord is everlasting God, the creator of the end of the earth. He will not grow tired or weary, and his understanding one can fathom. He gives strength to the weary and increases the power of the weak. Even youths grow tired and weary, and the young men stumble and fall; but those who love the Lord will renew their strength. They will soar with wings like eagle; they will run and not grow weary, they will walk and not faint"* (Isaiah 40:28-31).

If you are the one who is bringing stress to your partner by not doing what you are supposed to do, go to a place where you can be alone with God. Kneel down or stand and raise your hands and ask the Spirit of the living God to fall a fresh on you. Believe that God is with you and will give you strength and will of service your partner in love. He will fill your marriage with peace, love and joy and compassion.

8. Luck of compassion

Most of the persons who abuse their partners do so due to lack of compassion. The abuse may be physical or verbal. It can be in a form of passive aggression which employs silence as a weapon. Normally the abuser has no sympathy for his/her partner. Most of the cause of coldness is spiritual bankruptcy. It emanates from a soul without God. Thus, the secret of developing the spirit of empathy, consideration and kindness is to let God in your life.

If you are not compassionate, there is a way of developing this precious quality. Remember of an incident when your partner was in crisis. Put yourself in her shoes and cultivate the feelings to the point of tears. Do this exercise several times and then connect your feeling to your partner. You need also to remember that whenever Jesus did an act of mercy- healing and feeding- he was first moved by compassion. And thus, a Christian without compassion is a Christian without Christ. He is a contradiction in terms. Also, remember the golden rule: Do to others as you would like them do unto you. Do to your partner as you would like her/him do you. This includes allowing her/him to be and to become.

9. *Not allowing each other to be and to become.*

It has been rightly said: "no one crosses the same river twice." While there is something in personality that remains the same, there is another aspect which is constantly becoming. We are affected by our experiences and our ever-changing environment. The marriage partner who was a matriarch in the morning of their lives may become a follower in the afternoon or the twilight of their lives. The listener may become a talker while the talker may prefer to be a listener. There are also some changes which are caused by sickness. One partner may become depressed or even have a mental breakdown or may have an accident and lose a part of his body. One who had a high sex drive may have a declined sexual desire or sublimate to other activities. Most divorces occur when the major change occurs in one partner. I remember a parishioner who was in his second marriage informing me that he divorced when his wife became depressed and hospitalized. Some years later, I met him with the second wife and he quickly came to me and informed me that his second wife was having dementia.

One of Secrets of success is to embrace the new person. This includes a partner who is suffering from depression and other mental sicknesses. In marriage vows, we promise we will love, comfort, honor and keep and to hold each other: "For better for worse, for richer or poorer, in sickness and in health, to love and cherish, until we are parted by death."

As God continues working in your inner being, make every effort to appreciate your partner and vocalize your appreciation. Make this a daily routine. This practice will fill your life with peace, joy and love. It will lead to agape- love which gives and receives.

10. One partner being a parasite

The other cause of failure is when one partner is **a taker**. Interesting the Kikuyu name for uninitiated boy is a taker *(kahii)*. The word Kahii also means one who takes without giving. In North American, a partner who takes without giving is known as "a dead beat." In a seminar which we held in Nakuru, violence was identified as one of the challenges facing marriage today. Surprisingly, it was noted that more women are beating up the husbands. These are particularly the husbands who are alcoholic. They are beaten by their wives when they are drunk. In a Kenyan comedy show, a husband who has lost one eye during the fight argued that the government should have a law protecting these husbands and that they should be categorized with handicapped. Of course, these husbands need treatment and rehabilitation and training for job so that they may be asset to their wives rather than a liability. If you are the one who is taking without giving, know that there is an answer to this problem. Jesus is the answer. If you if you fully commit yourself to Christ. Jesus will end the desire to beer and drug. After the being filled with the Spirit of Christ, you will be a giver rather than a taker. Remember what the Bible says: *"It is more blessing to give than to receive."* Basically, everyone has something to give. If you are in between jobs and you are not bringing any income, you can give yourself to the working partner by doing most of the house chore. By thanking her for what she is and what she is doing.

11. **Bad Habits are** another cause of marriage strife. This ruinous habit includes not taking care of the home, and home steads, using the utensils without washing them or even removing them from the table, being dirty and fighting over a minute thing. The couple's inability to make a conscious decision not to argue over petty things, nagging, and being critical and leaving the messes for the other to clean. They get into negative patterns of relating and fall into lazy personal habits. All these behaviors bring strife in marriage and can lead to separation and divorce.

To deal with this problem, the partners should be conscious (even if it is one partner) of the problem and make every effort to change. Christian conduct is the answer. This is summarized by Paul as: *"Whatever is true, whatever is noble, whatever is right, whatever pure, whatever is lovely, whatever is admirable- if anything is excellent or praiseworthy-think about such things"* (Philippians 4:8).

In conclusion, to avoid failure, you need three keys to success: forgiving, giving and thanksgiving. Don't go to bed with anger and unforgiving spirit. Forgive your partner even if he /she hasn't asked for forgiveness. The Bible advises us not to "let the sun go down with your anger." Our Master taught us to pray "forgive us our sin as we forgive those who sin against us." To give means to be useful to your partner. As you get out of bed, ask yourself: "how am I going to be useful to partner today? If I am only for myself; what am I and if not now when?

Show your appreciation to your partner. Do not take her for granted. Acknowledge what he/she has done. This includes the regular house chores. Praise God for gift of your partner.

Praise God for what He is and what he has done for you. Form a habit of saying the general thanksgiving together:

> We pray, give us such an awareness of your mercies,
> That with truly thankful heart we may show forth your praise,
> Not only with our lips, but in our lives,
> By giving up ourselves to your service,
> And by walking before you in holiness and righteousness all our days;
> Through Jesus Christ our Lord, to whom, with you and the Holy Spirit,
> Be honor and glory throughout all ages. Amen
> (The Book of Common Prayer, New York: Church Pension Fund, 1979) p.101

12. Private affairs (Mpango *wa Kado)*

As noted above, one of the causes of marital problem are private affairs. As I discussed with several people in Kenya about the recent bill which legalized polygamous marriage, I learned that the law makers with private affairs were the one who introduced and supported the bill. I was privileged to watch the closing argument which was broadcasted by KTN. The law maker argued: "When the first wife is coming; she must know that the second is on way; and when the second is coming, she must know that the third is in the way." This meant that the second one will come without the consent of the first wife. When this bill was signed, I became sick to the stomach. The following day I asked one of our faculty whether he would give me pastoral counseling. But he thought that I was joking because I am Chancellor and professor of pastoral counseling. I felt disorientated because the Great Mother (see my book Initiation *and Pastoral Psychology:* a chapter of Great Mother) was wounded. This was due to the fact that I have positive influence from women in my life. The first impartation came from my mother whose was called in our village, WA Gatungu (of Gatungu- Gatungu being my given name). Being named after her father she was calling me Baba (Father) when I was growing. Besides building my ego, she was very proud of her children. When my father died (I was eight years old and she was thirty years old), the local chief wanted to marry her but she refused and said: "My children will never be second class citizens." She single handedly worked so hard to raise us even during the difficult times. She succeeded in producing a Canon, a Rural Dean, two bishops who are doctors of theology and a grandson who is PhD in Engineering. She survived my father for 56 years. She was so significant to us that we gave her a title of Honorable. My two elder sisters, Jail and Mary had positive influence on me. I remember one incident when I was five years old, we were herding with Mary while a young man who was older than her approaching me. Mary thought that he was trying to hurt her brother. She hit him with a club on the forehead and the blood gushed from his face. The other incident took place when saw a woman in a form of an angel, when my friend and me were crossing Maragua River- He was nine and I was seven years old. We underestimated the flood. When we were in the middle of the river we were being engulfed with water which was pushing us to the deep. At a nick of time, before we were totally submerged, I saw a lady holding my hand, I then held the hand of my friend, and the young woman miraculously took us to the riverbank. If this young woman had not rescued us, you could not read this book. Now you can see why I was sick when our mothers were dehumanized by the law makers in Kenya. Our augment is that women are not weak objects. This argument is supported by what I saw in Kenya in my recent mission. I saw women holding important positions in the government. I saw women in police uniforms, with machine guns protecting the country against Al- shabab. It is axiomatic that women are not weak and less tactful. KTN recently broadcasted as story of a man who was beating his wife. The wife run away but left the man with a shrinking male organ. The man was pleading with his wife publicly to come back and restore his sexual organ.

Another example of women's strength is demonstrated by, Meriam Ibrahim, who was condemned while eight months pregnant, to be flogged a hundred time and then to be executed for Marrying a Christian man, while her dad who abandoned them when she was a child, was a Muslim. She was put in a prison cell with her twenty-month Martin, awaiting to deliver and then be flogged and hanged. She stood firm in Christ and was ready to die for her marriage and her faith in Christ. She was forsaken by her brothers. One of her brothers said: "it's one of two; if she repents and returns to our Islamic faith and to the embrace of our family, then we are her family and she is ours,' but if she refuses, she should be executed.'"

Meriam experienced great pain for not only being forsaken by her family, but also giving birth in shackles. Yet she stood firm in her faith in Christ and her husband Wani. Her heroine action became global. Amnesty International condemned the sentence against Ibrahim, calling it 'abhorrent,' and the U.S. State Department said it was 'deeply disturbed' by the sentence. Finally, due to international pressure, Merian was released and flew to Italy with Italia Airlines, and had a blessing of shaking hands with Pope Francis.

When we honor women, we honor our mothers and sisters and ourselves. We respect that part of ourselves which I term *Great Mother* which creates and repairs human relationships. She helps us to reach out, to join and get in touch with, and be involved in concrete feelings, things and people. She is the source of life and nourishment. It is our prayer that our mothers and sisters will be emancipated. We also pray that Kenya will have strong prophetic voices and strong Christian politicians who will have this barbaric law repealed. As we have argued, the Bible makes it clear that marriage is between one man and one woman. It is also unhealthy for one partner to have extramarital sexual intercourse. The partners must be faithful to each other whether they have children or not.

It would be unfair to end this section without speaking for husbands. In the above-mentioned seminar which was held in Nakuru, Kenya, it was reported that there are more wives who are beating their husbands. They particularly beat them when they are drunk. This action is not justifiable. Alcoholism is a decease and for that reason the man needs rehabilitation and treatment. The church needs to have a group which is trained in intervention which would help the family in convincing the man to join Alcoholic Anonymous. Being a father of many nations, I have dealt with the causes of abused husband by the wives of different nations. Among the Mexicans who were members of the church, women who were in leadership fought or kicked their husbands when they were unemployed or were unable to bring enough money. One parishioner told me that his wife repeated the words "you have to go," so often that his five-year son would say to him: "Dad, you have to go, but I love you." Finally, when the wife's financial situation improved, the man was expelled from the house.

Among the African Americans whom I passionately ministered for twelve years, generally speaking, husbands were treated as eternal boys. At one time I called a man who was a parishioner, when he picked the phone, the wife who held the other phone was the first to answer for her husband and would not even allow the husband to speak with his pastor.

Wives of the Sudanese in diaspora whom we have ministered with lot of dedication and self-sacrifice, routinely call the police whenever there is a conflict between them and their husband. Whoever this happens, it is the husband who is handcuffed. As I write this page, Mama Mary has just given pastoral care to our priest who was visited by the police as he was just leaving for the church. His wife who is psychotic and has moved to another state called the police and lied to them that his husband was molesting his children. Before they had to handcuff him, he informed them that the woman is insane, and he showed them the court order which forbade the mother from being closer to the children. If this innocent husband didn't have the letter from the court, he could have been booked and leave behind the children whom he dearly loves.

In Western Kenya, it is reported that women in power are routinely raping men. There was a story which was reported in the local media of a male student who was given a ride by a lady. When he entered the car, he was given a snack. Instead of being taken to his destination, he was taken to a hotel. By the time they reached the hotel, the young man was drugged. The woman spent a night with the boy and left him alone, drugged with his sexual organ still erected. The boy was taken to the hospital by the police women who deal with these cases of the boys who are raped by women.

The above illustrations surface to show that many husbands are victims. As we have argued for husbands who are the head of their family, women in leadership should honor and love their husbands as Christ loved the church despite of its imperfection. When they let Christ in their lives, they will have Christ's love. This is what Jesus says about this love: "My commandment is this: Love each other as I have loved you. Great love has no one like this that he lays down his life for his friends." When father is dehumanized, the community lose vital qualities which are the substance of the Great Father. These qualities include wisdom, initiative, assertiveness, creativity and objectivity. (For more information see *Initiation and Pastoral*

Psychology in a chapter about the Great Father). Married partners with this love will embrace each other whether they have children or not.

12 Children

Children or lack of them can bring strain in marriage. When the couple stay without a child, there is pressure both from them and the extended family. When children come they can also be potential source of problem. Each partner comes with different family experiences, blessing and taboos. At a time, the differences while they are a source of conflict, they are also commentary. For instance, to rear a balance person, there is a need for control and freedom. One parent may be a dispenser of control while the other sees freedom as an ideal. The other area of conflict is support. One parents may regard the highest support as an ideal while the other prefer less support. The parents who have these opposing attitudes need to know that the children require bother freedom and control. If a child is over-controlled, the ego is weakened and will have problem to function is the society. If they have no control at all, they may become delinquents. Thus, the parents need to give each other freedom and make every effort to balance each other. However, having children can bring additional stress into a marriage because caretaking of children requires more responsibility as well as a change in roles, provides more fodder for disagreement and strain, and reduces the amount of time available for bond as a couple.

How to be a blessing to yourself and to the children.

i. Have time alone. This is the time when you enjoy each other and make the rules of how discipline and rear the kids and to enjoy yourself.

ii. Respect each other's view point remembering that each method has a positive effect on the children.

iii. When children try to separate you remind them: Your mom is my wife and the Bible advises you to honor your mother and father-This is a commandment with a promise that you will live well on earth. I am also admonished that I should love my wife as Christ loves the church. Your Dad is my husband the Bible requires that I love him and you are advised to honor and obey him.

iv. Be firm but not too serious with your children. Have fun and pray and read the Word of God with them.

Do realize that children were created with free will and one of their desires is to be different from their parents. They like occupying the empty space.

v. Know that like a prodigal son, they go through lostness particularly during their teenage (see *Initiation and Pastoral Psychology*- a chapter on lostness. When this is taking place remember a Swahili proverb: *asiyepotea haijui njia*- He who does not get lost does not know the way.

vi. Do not blame each other because of the shortcoming of your children. Remember David, the King after God's heart had Amon who raped his sister and Absalom who tried to overturn his father's government. Monica had Augustine who following the wrong company but later became one of the Church fathers, a Bishop and a Saint.

vii. If you don't have children. Adopt. The adopted children may even be more bonded to you than biological children. Remember Jesus was adopted by Joseph.

viii. Be contented with each other and with your children. As Saint Paul puts it: contentment with godliness is a great gain. *"And we know that in all things God works for good of those who love Him, who has been called according to His purpose"* (Romans 8:28).

CHAPTER THIRTY
REARING CHILDREN IN A TECHNOLOGICAL SOCIETY

Rearing children in a technological society poses great challenge to the married partners. The couples and their counsellors should bear in mind that personality is shaped by three factors:

1. Heritage. This include the genes of the parents and ethnic cultural heritage which is embedded in mythology, language of the tribe which is sub-symbolic universe of meaning of the tribe.

2. Environment. This include home, school, church, mass media, peer pressure. The media will include phonograph, information about how to get drug and alcohol and how to join terror groups. Parents cannot fully control their children from media.

3. Self-determination- Humans were given freedom of choice. As someone has puts "we are condemned to make choices." Remember even if you decide not to make a choice; you have made a choice. As Adler puts it: "You are either moving toward useful or useless destination." When teen decide to take drugs, they are traveling toward useless destination. This brings stress in marriage. The married partners need to hold hands together instead of blame game.

Those in diaspora do have extra challenges in that an individual is overprotected- you cannot use a cane. The proverb: "spare the rod spoil the child," is irrelevant in USA.

Children know their rights before they know how to become responsible. The consequence is prolonged adolescence. Children continue being a burden to their parents until late in their twenties. Others may remain deadbeat for life. In this case, the married partners should continue to love one another and to talk to and pray for their children without enabling their bad habit by giving them money.

As a Diaspora, beer in mind that if your children were born in Western Hemisphere they speak the language without accent. By having accent, they may think that they are more sophisticated in the western way of life than their parents. As a parent don't feel inferior. But remember your children don't have the blessings of facing challenges which you went through when you were growing Your Character was built by poverty, Hunger, war, safe and unsafe environments. This build up your character and in the words of Booker T Washington: "Character is power."

Lack of puberty rite of passage which enabled teens to move from childhood to adulthood contributes to postmodern problems which is characterize by additions, teen pregnancy, tattoos, bad behavior and wasting of time. Adolescence is one of the most challenging stage in life. Wayne Rise has written a book which is entitled *"HELP! THERE IS A TEENAGER* IN THE HOUSE." Teenage is a challenge to both the teens and their parents. They experience tension between childhood and adulthood; Independence VS dependence; Adolescent and his/her pear group; ethics and sexual urges; self-identity VS role confusion. (For more information see. John Githiga: Initiation and Pastoral Psychology. Amazon.com)

Being different personality types, the parents are challenged differently. One parent may be a dispenser of freedom while the other install discipline; one parent my pay attention to ideal and what the child has not become; while the other focuses on the growing edge. While each of these opposing attributes are useful to the child they bring tension between the married partners. Father and mother should equip themselves with three keys to success: forgiving; thanksgiving; giving. They have to forgive each other and forgive their children. The partners need to consistently appreciate one another and compliment their children for whatever they do. As the couple who whose secret of success is fifty, fifty, each partner must work hard to support the family. Children need to be trained to do their chores. These will train them to be contributing members of the family and the society.

You also need to continue instructing and guiding your children. Do turn you home to a war zone. Choose your battle carefully- don't burn your energy with small thing. It is not a big deal when a teen doesn't come to the dinner table on time.

More importantly, as parents, have time for yourself- discuss how you are going to deal with the children realizing that there are things which are beyond your control and beyond their control. Love one another, love your children. In Paul's words:

"Love is patient and kind; it is not easily angered; it keeps no records of wrong, it always protects, always trust, always hope, and always persevere." I Corinthian 13:4-7

CHAPTER THIRTY-ONE
FOR THOSE WHO INTEND TO MARRY

This chapter is for those who are making a choice for a partner in marriage. If you are looking for a long-life partner, you need to realize that this decision is one of the most important decisions in your life. For your partner will constitute seventy-five per cent of your environment. The is why the book of Common prayer advises: "The union of husband and wife in heart, body, and mind is intended by God for their mutual joy, for the help and comfort given one another in prosperity and adversity; and, when it is God's will, for the procreation of children and their nurture in the knowledge and love of God. Therefore, marriage is not to be entered into unadvisedly or lightly, but reverently, deliberately, and in accordance with the purpose for which it was instituted by God." (The Book of Common Prayer. The Seabury Press, 1979). You need to know your partner well. Most of the time, if know the person long enough, in good time and bad time, what you see is what you get. Most of the broken marriages are caused by either looking for the wrong things or for not knowing the partner at all. Some make choice based on physical attraction. He looks good and he has potential. You need to realize that character is formed very early in life. A big secret of our success in marriage is that Mary and I knew each other for nine years before marriage. Before we ever thought of engagement she knew who I was and she knew exactly what she was looking for. And what she saw is what she has been living with for forty-six years: She was looking for some who loves God, who goes to Church, who is faithful and could not ask for sex before marriage. I was also looking for a girl who loves God, who is involved in the church, hospitable and a nurturer. What surprises me is that the character I saw is the very character that I have lived with.

We used to attend early prayer in our church regularly. We still wake up before dawn for prayers and meditation. She was in the choir and she was one who gave a tune. She still does the same in our Church. She was very much involved in children ministry. She was a Sunday school teacher. She still works with children. We attended youth camp together. Even now at in her sixties she still ministers in youth camp. When she was a teenager, she was taking care for her terminally ill god father; she still ministers the terminally ill through hospice as a volunteer. She does this regularly and without any salary. She had a good relationship with her father. When she was a little girl, her father who was a business man, required Mary to visit him before any other child for he regarded her as his "lucky bird." Of course, Mary builds his ego. She has done the same to me and to the men in our church.

Thus, if you make a bad choice, you will pay a great price. If you make a wise choice you will have a successful marriage. This why it is important know your friend well. Know his/ her parents as well and how she relates to them. More importantly you need to seek God's guidance. A story is told of a teacher who loved two girls equally and had difficulty deciding whom to marry. He called each of them privately and asked. "In your marriage whom would you put first, your husband or God? The first answered: "I would put my husband first." The second responded; "I would put God first." The teacher decided to marry the one who put God first. And consequently, they had a successive marriage.

To get a godly partner, you must be godly. Which means being devoted to God and to building up the kingdom of God. I am awed by the way Mary has kept the same devotion to God and as she did before she ever knew that she will be marriage to a preacher. If you and your future partner are spiritual, you both have the fruit of the Holy Spirit which is essential to all relationship: *"The fruit of the spirit is love, joy, peace, patience, kindness, goodness, faithfulness, gentleness and self-control. Against such things there is no law."* Galatians 5:22-23.

CONCLUSION

To this end, it is evident that the secrets of success in marriage relationship included honoring and obey the leader whether it is a husband or a wife. Obedience is not weakness. Jesus was obedient to the Father. As Paul puts it: *"He humbled himself and became obedience to death even the death on the cross."* One who is leading must love his partner as Christ loved the church. The leader should not be bossy. The partners should stick together and be faithful to each other with mutual respect and love. They have to work hard on their marriage and be devoted to each other a hundred per cent. They also need to enjoy each other and have fun. They need three Keys to success- forgiving, giving, thanksgiving. To be successful and fruitful, the partners must put Christ in the center for all things were created by him and for him and it is in him that all things hold together (Colossians 1:15-20). when Christ is in the center, the couples conduct themselves in according to Christian ethics which is summarized by Saint Paul this way: *"whatsoever in true, whatsoever is noble, whatsoever is right, whatsoever is pure, whatsoever is lovely, whatsoever is admirable-if anything is excellent and praiseworthy-think about such things. And the peace of God which transcends all understanding, will guard your hearts and minds in Christ Jesus* (Philippians 4:7-8).

www.ingramcontent.com/pod-product-compliance
Lightning Source LLC
LaVergne TN
LVHW040156080526
838202LV00042B/3183